A COMPREHENSIVE GUIDE TO MERGERS & ACQUISITIONS

A COMPREHENSIVE GUIDE TO MERGERS & ACQUISITIONS

MANAGING THE CRITICAL SUCCESS FACTORS ACROSS EVERY STAGE OF THE M&A PROCESS

Yaakov Weber
Shlomo Y. Tarba
Christina Öberg

Vice President, Publisher: Tim Moore
Associate Publisher and Director of Marketing: Amy Neidlinger
Executive Editor: Jeanne Glasser Levine
Managing Editor: Kristy Hart
Project Editor: Andy Beaster
Copy Editor: Apostrophe Editing Services
Proofreader: Anne Goebel
Indexer: Larry Sweazy
Cover Designer: Alan Clements
Senior Compositor: Gloria Schurick
Manufacturing Buyer: Dan Uhrig

FT Press offers excellent discounts on this book when ordered in quantity for bulk purchases or special sales. For more information, please contact U.S. Corporate and Government Sales, 1-800-382-3419, corpsales@pearsontechgroup.com. For sales outside the U.S., please contact International Sales at international@pearsoned.com.

Printed in the United States of America

First Printing December 2013

ISBN-10: 0-13-301415-0
ISBN-13: 978-0-13-301415-0

Pearson Education LTD.
Pearson Education Australia PTY, Limited.
Pearson Education Singapore, Pte. Ltd.
Pearson Education Asia, Ltd.
Pearson Education Canada, Ltd.
Pearson Educación de Mexico, S.A. de C.V.
Pearson Education—Japan
Pearson Education Malaysia, Pte. Ltd.

Library of Congress Control Number: 2013949964

To:

Alice, for friendship and support

Dania, Ohad, and Tahel, for giving my life meaning and comic relief

To the memory of my mother, Otilia

*Thanks you for being there for me the time or two that I have fallen behind.
I'll always be there for you, too.*

—Y. W.

To the memory of my father, Ruslan,

who is always in my heart.

—S. Y. T.

Contents

About the Authors

Yaakov Weber, Ph.D. is a professor of management at the School of Business Administration, College of Management, Rishon Lezion, Israel, and president of the strategic management consulting firm Strategy, Implementation, Results. He has practiced as a strategic management consultant for more than 25 years and has assisted executives of numerous companies in successfully managing various stages of domestic and international mergers and acquisitions, including planning, negotiation, and integration. He lectures at various universities in the United States, Western and Eastern Europe, and China, in graduate schools of business administration as well as executive programs. He has conducted numerous workshops to top executives in many countries.

Dr. Weber's studies have been published in top international academic and practitioner journals, and his papers have received more than 2,000 citations in leading journals and books. He is the winner of the 2010 Outstanding Author Contribution Award.

Professor Weber is co-founder and co-president of the EuroMed Research Business Institute (www.emrbi.com), the EuroMed Academy of Business, and the EuroMed Research Centre. EMRBI performs a variety of international academic and business activities (conferences, business research, teaching, training programs, and so on) that involve businesses and consultants in, and related to, the EuroMed region.

Shlomo Y. Tarba, Ph.D. is a lecturer in Strategic Management and Global Strategic Partnerships at the Management School, The University of Sheffield, UK. He received his Ph.D. from Ben-Gurion University and master's degree in biotechnology at the Hebrew University of Jerusalem, Israel. His research papers has been published in journals such as *Academy of Management Perspectives, International Studies of Management & Organization, Thunderbird International Business Review, International Journal of Cross-Cultural Management, Human Resource Management Review, Advances in Mergers and Acquisitions*, and others. Dr. Tarba has served as a guest editor for the special issues on Strategic Agility at *California Management Review*; Organizational Ambidexterity at *Human Resource Management*; Maturing Born-Global Knowledge Intensive Firms at *Management International Review*; Emotions, Culture, and Stress in the Interorganizational Encounters at *International Business Review*; and others. He was granted the 2010 Outstanding Author Contribution Award by Emerald Publishing. His consulting experience includes biotechnological and telecom companies, as well as industry associations such as The Israeli Rubber and Plastic Industry Association and The U.S.–Israel Chamber of Commerce.

Christina Öberg, Ph.D. is an associate professor at the Department of Industrial Management and Logistics, Lund University. She currently conducts research at the Centre for Innovation and Service Research, University of Exeter. She received her Ph.D. in industrial marketing from Linköping University. She has an industry background in which she held such positions as financial manager and head accountant. Her research interests include mergers and acquisitions, brands and identities, customer relationships, and innovation management. She has previously been published in journals such as *Journal of Business Research*, *Construction Management and Economics*, *International Journal of Innovation Management*, *European Journal of Marketing*, *The Service Industries Journal*, *Journal of Business-to-Business Marketing*, *Scandinavian Journal of Management*, *Thunderbird International Business Review*, and *Industrial Marketing Management*.

Preface

One of the enduring paradoxes in merger and acquisition (M&A) activity has been the propensity of corporations and executives to engage in M&As despite consistent evidence that post-merger performance of acquiring firms is disappointing. For example, in 2011, global M&A activity shattered previous years' deal volume records, and recent surveys reveal that despite the financial market crisis, executives remain upbeat about their M&A plans around the world (Deloitte 2012; Bloomberg 2012). However, the success of the M&A remains questionable. For example, managers of acquiring firms report that only 56 percent of their acquisitions can be considered successful against the original objectives set for them (Schoenberg 2006). A possible explanation to this paradox is that existing knowledge on M&As provides a limited and insufficient understanding of different parts of this important phenomenon. For instance, it is possible that top executives might perceive an M&A as a good step for corporate growth at the pre-merger stage, but poorly implemented during the post-merger process. Despite their popularity, M&As remain poorly understood and poorly executed.

This book is about developing a better knowledge on how to make an M&A work. We have written this book as a comprehensive guide to help executives and managers to navigate a successful M&A. Thus, the book provides a general framework that describes all stages of the M&A in which actions and processes are explained versus major problems confronting managers who plan and execute the M&A.

This book is grounded in both experience and research on many firms and in many industries. During the last 30 years, we have conducted research on the factors that lead to value creation in the M&A. At the same time, we accumulated experience in consulting to executives about various stages of M&As and developed managerial tools to deal with various challenges at the M&A planning, negotiation, and post-merger integration (PMI) stages.

There are several main advantages of this book. First and foremost, it does not only look at all M&A stages, but also at the essential interrelationships between them. Thus, such activities as comparing M&A alternatives, planning, negotiating, and choosing an M&A, for instance, depends, in addition to financial and strategic factors, on the implementation challenges. Thus, a buyer can use, after assessment, the integration process challenges expected during the PMI stage, for instance, in negotiation of price, terms, and processes, before the deal is signed, as well as level and duration of payments based on the accomplishment of some objectives after the deal.

Second, a review of scholarly and practitioner-focused writing on M&As reveals that important topics have been occasionally mentioned only in passing. Even in those cases in which important subjects were mentioned, not many details were presented on how these issues make a difference and how to use them for M&A success. Therefore, this book elaborates and articulates on many neglected, but essential, topics, such as the use of cultural differences in all M&A stages, trust, leadership, Human Resource practices, communication, and more that other scholars and practitioners recognize but have not developed.

Finally, the highly dismal performance track record of M&As might stem from a lack of synchronization between different M&A process stages. The framework suggested in Chapter 2, "An Integrated Model for Value Creation in Mergers and Acquisitions," and elaborated through different chapters, provides tools to synchronize all M&A stages, actions, and processes. Our hope is that this book can reduce the failure rate of M&As and increase M&As' success so that they can reach their potential.

References

Bloomberg 2012 global M&A outlook. (2012). Report.

Deloitte. (2012). Growth through M&A: Promise and reality. Report.

Schoenberg, R. (2006). Measuring the performance of the corporate acquisitions: An empirical comparison of alternative metrics. *British Journal of Management*, 17, 361-370.

PART I

Value Creation Model for Mergers and Acquisitions

1

THE M&A PARADOX: FACTORS OF SUCCESS AND FAILURE IN MERGERS AND ACQUISITIONS

Why do experienced senior managers fail again and again in mergers and acquisitions (M&A)?[1] For example, in a well-documented case, Daimler had to separate from Chrysler, which it had purchased approximately 10 years before, after continuous losses of billions of dollars. And in another case that was widely covered in newspapers, in October 2007, Patricia Russo, the CEO of the Alcatel-Lucent merger, admitted that after three sequential profit warnings, the results of the merger were lower than expected (*The Associated Press*, October 31, 2007). In contrast, few companies succeed persistently in M&A, such as Heinz, Unilever, and Electrolux.

Does the success of a few companies explain the continuous increase in the number of M&A? The main drivers for M&A relate to various growth opportunities such as acquiring new products, expansion into new geographical areas, or access to new customers. This is in addition to such motives as improving profitability and the company's strategic capabilities and positioning. Thus, there is no surprise that the activity of M&A in 2011 showed continued recovery from the downturn of 2008 and 2009, despite the U.S. debt downgrade, Europe's ongoing debt crisis, and heightened worries about global economic conditions.

Many research studies conducted over the decades clearly show that the rate of failures is at least 50 percent. In surveys conducted in recent years, the percentage of companies

---

1   The term *merger* refers generally to a "merger between equals" and *acquisition* refers to the situation in which the management of the acquiring company controls the acquired company. Experience shows that even if a "'merger between equals" is declared, within days or weeks it is clear to each one of the parties who is controlling and who is being controlled. This book therefore does not make any distinction between these terms and uses them interchangeably.

that failed to achieve the goals of the merger reached 83 percent. Following these findings, it can be expected that senior managers and boards of directors would avoid merger and acquisition activities as much as possible and would search for other strategies to achieve market share and profitability goals. However, reality indicates the opposite. The trend of mergers and acquisitions has been constantly increasing over the past 20 years. Moreover, the number of mergers and acquisitions and the sums of money invested in them have shattered the all-time record almost every year!

Global M&A deal volume rose from 27,460 transactions in 2010 to 30,366 in 2011, an 11 percent increase according to WilmerHale report from 2012 on M&A activity. Similarly, global M&A deal value increased 53 percent to $3.11 trillion in 2011, up from $2.03 trillion in 2010. Average global deal size grew to $102.6 million in 2011, up from $73.8 million in 2010. In the United States, the volume of M&A activity was fairly steady, increasing 7 percent, from 9,238 transactions in 2010 to 9,923 in 2011. U.S. deal value jumped 79 percent, from $887.3 billion in 2010 to $1.59 trillion in 2011, due to a spate of large transactions.

In Europe, both deal volume and deal value continued to increase from their 2010 levels. Deal volume increased 15 percent, from 11,736 transactions in 2010 to 13,501 in 2011. Boosted by a number of large transactions, total European deal value increased 91 percent, from $780.5 billion to $1.49 trillion. The Asia-Pacific region also experienced growth in deal volume and value. The number of Asia-Pacific deals increased 12 percent, from 7,970 transactions in 2010 to 8,905 in 2011, whereas aggregate deal value increased 26 percent, from $652.5 billion to $822.2 billion. According to Bloomberg's M&A report from 2012, China's appetite for buying opportunities continued to increase, with $158 billion worth of deals announced in 2011, a moderate 9 percent increase from $145 billion in 2010.

And the forecast? According to a survey report of financial market professionals made by Bloomberg, the M&A activity will continue to grow. Asia-Pacific companies are expected to be the most aggressive buyers, whereas respondents expect the most attractive targets to be found among firms in the European region.

Yet, even if the number of mergers and acquisitions declines in the next few years, it is clear that this strategy will continue to remain important to many organizations. In addition, the increase of international activities and processes of globalization will encourage international mergers and acquisitions. Will the high rate of failures continue to characterize the M&A activities? It is hard to say. There are reasons to believe that certain dimensions of M&A remain difficult due to the complexity of M&A.

The primary reasons for failures is related to the fact that it is easy to buy but hard to perform an M&A. In general, many mergers and acquisitions are characterized by the lack of planning, limited synergies, differences in the management/organizational/ international culture, negotiation mistakes, and difficulties in the implementation of the strategy following the choice of an incorrect integration approach on the part of the merging organizations after the agreement is signed. Most failure factors indicate a lack of knowledge among senior managers for the management tools that enable coping with the known problems of M&A.

The sharp increase in M&A activities during the second half of the past century on the one hand, and the tremendous amount of failures on the other hand, draw research interests from different areas of business administration and economics. Each area of interest has a special point of view and different measures of success. This chapter describes the factors of success or failure in mergers and acquisitions according to three main areas: economics and finance, strategic management, and organizational behavior. The overarching theme of this book is that only the combination of knowledge from all these areas can bring M&A success.

Finance and the Capital Market

Researchers from economics and finance areas measure success by the change in the stock rates (with the reduction of industry fluctuations) in the first few days after the announcement of the merger. When the stocks rise, the merger is successful, and when the stock price falls, the merger is described as a failure. The basic assumption of economics/ finance scholars is that the stock value reflects the company value in an objective manner based on all the existing public information. The idea is that the immediate change in the stock price reflects changed expectations on the value of the firm, and thereby indicates a long-term trend. Therefore, they assert that every M&A that causes an immediate rise in the stock value (after the reduction for fluctuations in the capital market), reflects success and creates value for the stockholders. In contrast, a merger that causes the decline in the stock price in the first days after the announcement of the merger reflects failure and loss for the stockholders.

A conclusion accepted today, after decades of research, is that only stockholders of the acquired company profit, whereas the stockholders of the acquiring firm do not, on the average, receive any benefit from the merger. The main reason for failures, according to this perspective, is that the acquiring company pays a premium that reaches above the value of the acquired company. This premium is generally so high that even successful management activities after the acquisition do not provide return on investment and do not remedy the valuation "error." The capital market identifies this mistake and responds in the change of the stock price. For example, the stocks of AOL declined in the first 24 hours after the acquisition of Time Warner was announced. The assumption was that the price paid for Time Warner was very high and not justifiable. Its stocks continued to decline for many months after the acquisition. It should be noted though that the capital market's valuation makes mistake in many cases, such as the Daimler-Chrysler merger. In that case, the stock price rose immediately after the merger announcement. However,

---

2 years following it, the stock value declined to 50 percent of its value at the time of the merger.

It also becomes clear that the over-payment for acquisitions is a frequent problem also for other reasons. The personal interests of senior management are not always commensurate with those of the stockholders. The CEO and his peers see personal advantages in the merger, such as greater empowerment and control of a larger organization, improvement of the social-management status, and higher salaries and benefits. In addition, senior managers have the possibility of moving to the management of another company from an improved position following the merger because of the considerable experience that characterizes a larger company. In other words, one of the main reasons for the failures of M&A, according to finance and economics researchers, is the ego of the CEO and his management. One of the senior vice managers of the large pharmaceutical company Glaxo Welcome addressed this issue: "Ego has precedence over future strategies" (*Fortune*, March 1998). In other words, the personal considerations of senior managers precede rational considerations that are supposed to be expressed in the prior planning of the future strategies of the organization.

Another reason for failures, related to the ego of the CEO and the over-payment, is known as the *hubris hypothesis* or the *sin of pride*. This issue addresses the considerable self-confidence that a person has in his ability to overcome mishaps and succeed even when the chances are low. The concept is known from Aristotle's model of tragedy, in which successful and talented people suffer from pride or excessive self-confidence and thus fail. The tragedy is that they, more than other people, can avert the failure. Exactly like Icarus, who, according to Greek myth, despite his father's warnings, flew too high with his wax wings, which melted when he was too close to the sun—and he fell to the sea and drowned. In the Israeli version of the "Icarus" story, there are several expressions that indicate the sin of pride, such as "Trust me," "It will be alright," and "It won't happen to me." In other words, the CEO is certain that despite the over-payment, the merger/acquisition is worthwhile. He is certain that under his management and through integration of the organizations, effectiveness will increase, new options will be created, the performances of the acquired company will improve within a short period of time, and the advantages of the merger will be realized.

It should be noted that there are cases in which it became clear that the over-payment was worthwhile. When Electra was acquired by Elco, for instance, approximately 30 percent more than the worth, according to the stock value, was paid, but eventually it became clear that the acquisition was very beneficial, at least in the field of manufacturing and sales of air-conditioning units.

In any event, despite the lack of profitability of the acquiring companies, the activity of mergers and acquisitions continues to grow and break records. Why? Following are several possible explanations for this conundrum:

- One possibility is that although there is no potential for profit, the activity continues because

  1. Managers make mistakes in the evaluation of the value.

  2. Managers search to maximize their profit, even at the expense of the stockholders.

  3. Managers act out of pressure from the board of directors and stockholders to show continuous growth.

- Mergers have the potential for profit but

  1. Organizational problems that occur after the merger entail many costs that negate the potential profit or do not allow for the realization of the M&A.

  2. There is a methodological problem with the measurement of the success and profitability of mergers and acquisitions, and therefore the existing profitability is not evident.

  3. The M&A causes reactions among external stakeholders that offset possible positive consequence. Such reactions include how customers decide to change their ways of buying products, whereas a continuous cash flow from these customers was part of the valuation of the acquired party. It is possible that only certain types of mergers bring a profit to the stockholders, whereas others do not.

The reasons in the first preceding topic lead to two other areas that explain differently the factors of success and failure of mergers and acquisitions: strategic management and organizational behavior.

Strategic Management

Researchers from the field of strategic management focus on the management of the organization itself and its long-term planning. Strategic management does not accept the assumptions of economic/finance researchers and of the capital market approach that maintains that

- It is possible to precisely predict the future cash flow of the firm for a period of several years.

- There is the potential for increased inner effectiveness that is greater than the performance of the acquired party's managers.

The experience and knowledge that have accumulated in the realm of strategic management show that strategies change following the frequent environmental shifts and following implementation difficulties. Therefore, future cash flow, which constitutes a main basis for the value evaluation, is difficult to predict.

In addition, strategic management scholars maintain that the ability of inner improvement of effectiveness of the organization is limited, and at some stage, it may detrimentally influence its competitive ability. In contrast, the ideas advocated by economics/finance reseachers led at the end of the 1980s to a growth of hostile takeovers and leveraging using finance and LBO (acquisition of the company using the leveraging by managers and workers). Capital actors who adopted these methods believed that it was possible to increase the effectiveness of the organization and thereby boost its value. However, these hostile takeovers nearly vanished in the 1990s. In addition, it must be remembered that this economics/finance approach is influenced by the American capital market for the measurement of M&A success and emphasizes the short-term effects. In Japan and Europe, the tendency is to focus on performance and long-term strategic goals, and the measurements and reward systems are commensurate with this tendency.

The strategic management approach addresses a large number of measures of success, including the size of sales, the increase of the market share, the improvement of competitive abilities, and of course the change in profitability after the merger in relation to a period before the M&A. These measures are influenced, according to strategic management researchers, by the fit between the organizations, and therefore the main factor of success/failure in the merger/acquisition is the degree of strategic fit between the two companies. Strategic fit is expressed in the synergy potential ($2 + 2 = 5$) of the merger. (The topic of synergy will be discussed separately in Chapter 5, "Synergy Potential and Realization.") Simply put, there is synergy when it is possible to operate two business units more profitably when they are under the control of one factor than when each one operates separately. Strategic fit and synergy exist in the related merger in which the two organizations operate in the same industry or in related industries. The clearest example is the merger of competitors, when it is then possible to unite administrations and operative functions. Thus, it is possible to achieve the joint level of sales (or more than that) at lower costs, such as in the merger of Elco and Electra in the beginning 1990s in the field of air-conditioning units.

In contrast, when Elco acquired Shekem, which included a food chain and a clothing chain, the synergy was low (only evident in the area of the marketing of electronic products). This was similarly the situation in which a building contractor acquired the Pizza Hut chain. There was no potential for synergies, and the merger was defined as an unrelated merger. Some people asserted that there were synergies because Pizza Hut restaurants are situated in buildings. (Cynics maintained that the only synergy would be if pizzas were sold with a cement sauce.) These unrelated mergers did not succeed. The recommendation in the strategic management approach is unequivocal: Only synergetic mergers are recommended, and unrelated mergers should be avoided, with the exception of highly specific cases.

However, even in related mergers, the number of failures is high. Research conducted by Professor Michael Porter from Harvard examined the percentage of success among related mergers. The criterion of success/failure was the percentage of organizational divorce in a period of 5 years (and even more) after the merger/acquisition. The sample included large firms in the United States, and the basic assumption was that in related mergers, the intention is to maintain the acquired party for a long period of time to realize the synergy potential. In this sample, too, the percentage of divorce was high, above 50 percent. The conclusion was that a firm that is forced to resell a company it has acquired does so after several attempts to connect the organizations and to exploit the synergy, and when it finally despairs, after much suffering, it "vomits" the company. This was the case in the merger of Madge and the Israeli company Lannet. Lannet was acquired for 330 million dollars and was sold after approximately 3 years to Lucent for approximately 100 million dollars. The integration process of the organizations did not succeed. Madge's profits dropped, and its stock value reached approximately 5 percent of the value on the day of the merger.

Explanations to the miserable results of related mergers are that the potential of synergy is not always realized in the implementation. There are two main reasons for such lack of synergy realization. First, the synergy is not exploited because of lack of prior planning. Using prior planning, it is possible to avoid superfluous costs, to identify the main sources of synergy, and to enable the actualization of the synergy potential in a relatively short time frame. Without a defined plan, the potential of synergy melts away in long and complex organizational processes that do not bear fruit. (Part II, "Analysis Tools for Key Success Facgors," is dedicated to the process of planning.) The second reason for the lack of synergy realization in related mergers is linked to the lack of focus on human factors, namely, the managers and the workers, and then primarily those of the acquired company. This reason is the topic discussed under the title of organizational behavior next.

Organizational Behavior

Researchers and counselors from the field of organizational behavior maintain that the primary cause of failure in mergers and acquisitions is the lack of consideration of the human factor during the process of the planning and implementation of the merger. In other words, even given the conditions of success according to the first two areas, namely, payment appropriate to the acquired company's value and the M&A being conducted between two related organizations with the potential for synergy, the human factor might cause the merger failure. Managers and workers that do not adjust to the merger, consciously or subconsciously, as the consequence of cultural or management style differences, cause considerable costs and disable the exploitation of the synergy potential.

Following comprehensive research performed in recent years and the accumulated experience in many mergers, it is known that, in essence, the main factor that influences the managers and the workers, primarily in the acquired company, is the degree of the management/organizational culture differences between the two merging organizations. When the difference of the management culture is considerable, the merger is fated for failure. (Management/organizational culture differences exist between organizations in every field and in every country. International culture differences add to the difference that exists between the organizations.) Thus, the CEO of Daimler-Chrysler, the German Juergen Schrempp, maintained that the American James Holden did not succeed in adjusting to his management approach that includes, for example, a policy of cutting expenses and ongoing reporting of the important developments in Chrysler and thus induced ongoing uncertainty. Figure 1.1, which is based on research conducted in the United States and Israel including domestic and international mergers, explains the impact of cultural differences on acquisition success/failure.

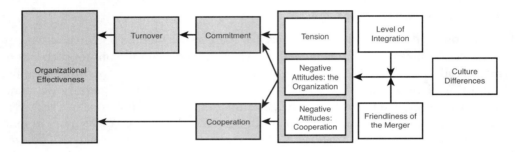

Figure 1.1   The Impact of the Management Culture Differences on the Success of Mergers and Acquisitions

This figure indicates that the culture differences cause tension/pressure and negative attitudes among managers and workers, primarily those of the acquired company. Following the tension and negative attitudes toward the acquiring organization, the commitment of the managers to the success of the merger is impaired. In addition, the level of cooperation between the two sides greatly declines. Thus, senior managers in the acquired company abandon the company and move to competitors or to other firms. This departure of managers, most of which occurs in the first year after the merger, is found in research studies to be related to the decline in the financial performances of the merger.

It is not surprising that Amos Michelson, the owner of the Canadian Company Creo, which purchased the preprinting division of the Israeli company Scitex, said, 1 year after the acquisition was completed that "This merger is not a simple task." Indeed, 20 of the 25 senior managers of Scitex left in the first year after the merger because they did not want to adjust to the management style of Creo. At the end of that year, Michelson admitted that the return to the pace of growth of 30 percent a year that characterized Creo before the merger would occur only several years later. Actually, the company never returned to these performances.

The problem of the departure of managers and key personnel is especially exacerbated among hi-tech companies. In these companies, the professional knowledge is held by the people, and the ability to develop and innovate is also related to the interaction among the people on the research and development teams. In essence, a main reason for the acquisition is the innovativeness, professional knowledge, and talented personnel. If managers and key personnel leave the acquired company, then the acquiring company is left without the value that it paid for. It is not surprising that such mergers/acquisitions are doomed to fail, especially if the cultural differences and their influences are not identified and analyzed ahead and treated immediately, before, during, and after the papers are signed. This, of course, is important in every industry and in every area.

Indeed, Eli Horowitz, the previous chairman of the Board of Teva, which, due to M&A, has become the world's largest generic pharmaceutical company, noted that "When companies are merged, it is possible to transfer a productive line but the organizational culture is difficult to transfer."

References

The Associated Press, October 31, 2007

Fortune, March 1998

Porter, M. E. (1985). Competitive advantage: *Creating and sustaining superior performance*. New York: Free Press.

WilmerHale 2012 M&A report. (2012). Wilmer Cutler Pickering Hale and Dorr Llp. www.wilmerhale.com.

Weber, Y. and Tarba, S. Y. (2011). Exploring integration approach in related mergers. Post-merger integration in the high-tech industry. *International Journal of Organizational Analysis*, 19 (3), 202-221.

2

AN INTEGRATED MODEL FOR VALUE CREATION IN MERGERS AND ACQUISITIONS

Overview

The previous chapter provides some explanations derived from different disciplines and domains of knowledge and research on M&A success and failure factors. Researchers and most consultants at each discipline, however, generally ignore the other knowledge and research streams and focus on a specific angle of the issue related to its background. Although some of the factors of success and failure are well known to experienced executives and consultants, dealing with some factors and ignoring other factors does not necessarily lead to a successful merger. Thus, the rate of failure remains high, as described in the previous chapter. This book suggests a multidisciplinary approach to understanding and managing M&A. Thus, this chapter provides a model for value creation in M&A that integrates the most updated knowledge accumulated in various disciplines and lists important steps needed for successful mergers based on several disciplines and research streams. Subsequent chapters elaborate on each step and on the critical connections between them.

Different Disciplines, Different Stages, No Interrelationships

There is a complex set of interrelationships between factors at the pre- and post-merger stages, such as strategic goals, synergy, corporate culture, national culture, integration approaches, leadership, communication, human resource management, to mention just a few, and the adaptation of practices during various stages, as well as their influence on the success of domestic and international mergers. Several independent streams of management research have studied either the *pre*-acquisition or the *post*-merger integration stage. For example, one stream examined the relationships between firm-level (macro-level) measures of financial performance and the strategic fit between buying and selling firms. These studies hypothesized, but failed to find, a consistent relationship between performance gains and the degree to which the merging firms share similar functions (et al. King, 2004). A second stream of research examined the cultural fit between buying and selling firms and its impact on the success of the combination (et al. Stahl and Voight, 2008), and a few studies examined the effects of M&A on the human factor (micro level), including the psychological effects on managers and employees. But these streams have paid little attention, for instance, to the human side and HR practices that lead to success and did not take international differences into account. Thus, high causal ambiguity exists before, during, and after the deal is signed.

The relationship between the levels and stages of the M&A process is by no means clear. The bodies of literature on M&A seem to exist in a state of splendid isolation. For example, it is difficult to find a study that investigates the effects of cultural differences in M&A on the planning of a merger, the screening of merger alternatives, or the negotiation phase. Studies on cultural differences usually focus on issues relevant to the post-merger stage, such as the integration of the two companies or the turnover of top executives after the deal is signed. Several scholars raised this issue years ago (et al. Chatterjee 1992, et al. Weber 1996, Weber and Tarba 2011, Weber and Fried 2011), but the situation has not changed much since then. Authors writing about macro- and micro-level variables in M&As or about the pre- and post-merger stages might share some definitions and terms, but by and large refrain from stepping onto each other's turf, thereby missing out on opportunities for cross-fertilization.

There are many factors that make M&A complex phenomenon, probably one of the most challenging managerial tasks. Because mergers occur relatively infrequently and unpredictably, the ability of management to accumulate the large amounts of *observations* needed to capitalize on simple mechanisms is limited. Moreover, mergers occur in heterogeneous forms, which are inherently causally ambiguous. Thus, much effort is needed to develop and update acquisition-specific methods, procedures, and systems that lower the degree of causal ambiguity between decisions, actions, and performance. Furthermore, the knowledge accumulated in many studies that were conducted under the assumption that M&A are homogeneous can not explicate in fact the important differences between M&A. In reality, not all M&As are alike. A major omission in this respect has been a focus on the cultural differences between the acquirer and target companies rather than on differences between the national cultures of acquirers from various countries. To continue the example of HR practices, comparisons of effects on the human side and HR practices in M&As that take place in different countries are rare. At the same time, globalization increases the number of cross-border M&As, with important consequences for human resources, such as motivation, turnover of acquired top executives, greater ethnic diversity, and altered psychological contracts between employers and employees. All these changes require a sophisticated adaptation of human resources to diverse situations in different countries and sectors. The failure to account for personnel issues educes the potential of Human Resource Management (HRM) to play an important role during *all* stages of M&A.

The focus on individual aspects of the merger process is also shared by practitioners. In many cases, M&As are initiated by top managers coming across an "opportunity," which was "discovered" in informal conversations with business people, by the approach of investment bankers acting as mediators, or by other means. Following preliminary discussions, the managers or owners request a valuation of the target company and negotiate mostly over the price. (*Horse trading* is a common term.) Only after reaching an agreement do many top managers begin thinking in-depth about the integration of the organizations. In many cases, they ask, too late, key managers, who were not involved in any of the early stages of the merger, to plan and implement the post-merger integration process. Often the top managers emphasize their anticipation for financial performance improvement in a short-term period, especially if payment for the acquired company turns out to be in excess of initial estimates.

In most cases, the managers involved in each stage come from different disciplines. For example, financial managers are typically involved in the early stages and human resource managers in the later ones. It is the overarching argument of this book that the separation between M&A process stages and professional managers coming from different disciplines reduces the likelihood of success of the merger process for two main reasons. First, the specialized knowledge of the managers of the organizational functions (R&D, marketing, production, HR, and so on) regarding the advantages and disadvantages of the merger is not integrated into the decision-making process. Consequently, the owners and top managers cannot evaluate accurately the synergic potential and added value of the merger. Synergy can be high in certain functions and low in others and requires thorough professional analyses. Managers of individual organizational units can evaluate more accurately the advantages and disadvantages of the acquired vis-à-vis the acquirer in the domain under their care as well as the true potential the merger can create in that domain. Furthermore, functional managers can estimate the costs and the obstacles of a merger to seize operational synergy as well as knowledge transfer from one organization to the other in their domain before the deal is signed. These estimates and data are crucial for all stages of M&A, including the planning, negotiation, and implementation of the merger. In their absence, decision makers might reject a good merger, pursue a flawed one, or pay high premium for the acquisitions.

Moreover, the activities surrounding an acquisition vary and are quite technically complex. Therefore, these activities require segmentation of the analytical tasks, such as industry analysis, product analysis, financial valuations, antitrust consideration, pension fund compatibilities, and more. The analyses of different experts and specialists that are usually sequential, temporal, isolated, and represent different perspectives are difficult to integrate. In many cases, the analyses focus on a few dominant paradigms that restrict considerations of nonstandard data, such as organizational cultural differences, and thus limit the decision-making process and eventually negatively affect the merger's performance.

Second, not involving managers at every stage of the decision-making process has clear negative consequences, such as a lack of motivation and a decreased commitment to success, both crucial factors in the integration process of the organizations. Post-merger integration and the exploitation of the synergy potential depend to a large extent on the cooperation, commitment, and motivation of the managers of different functions in the organization. In their absence, the merger is likely to fail.

Many top executives and owners assume that integration problems can be solved by increasing the satisfaction of the managers, that is, by raising their salaries by a certain amount. If this fails to achieve the expected results, so they assume, the managers can be easily replaced. Experience shows that most good managers are not moved even by a raise of several dozens' percent. On the contrary, they are worried by differences in corporate culture and the predicted changes in their work. Good managers have employment alternatives in competing companies or in other fields. Research indicates that a high percentage of good managers leave during the first year following the merger. In these cases, empirical evidence shows that the merger runs into many obstacles, and the acquirer's financial performance decreases. Finally, emphasis on instant financial results disregards the sequential stages of integration needed for the creation of value and the realization of synergy. Many managers and owners are unaware of the complexity of the integration problems, the need for a strategic and organizational analysis, and the need for a detailed long-term plan that takes many factors into account. Only thorough planning and implementation can bring the expected results. Insistence on achieving instant results (often the outcome of high payment for the acquisition and of criticism by stockholders) while disregarding the stages of the integration process can lead to rash actions that are liable to spoil the synergy potential that eventually can lead to failure of the merger.

To avoid such problems, it is important to implement a systematic M&A process. The model proposed in this chapter integrates knowledge from different disciplines and research streams and identifies the important steps and the interrelationships that must be taken into account when pursuing an M&A.

An Integrated Model for Value Creation in M&A

Research data and findings from various fields, as well as the knowledge that has accumulated from experience, indicate that conducting M&A is a complex process in which many factors determine success or failure. The process can be divided into three main interconnected stages:

- **Stage I**—Planning and strategic management
- **Stage II**—Negotiation, due diligence, and agreement
- **Stage III**—Implementation and post-merger integration

It is the approach of this book to focus on the connection among the three stages. For example, in the planning stage, you must consider the negotiation and implementation processes. Furthermore, the negotiations provide important information about the implementation process, the financial estimates, and the strategies of the acquired company. This information feeds the planning process, which eventually affects the negotiation and implementation processes. Figure 2.1 describes the process stages and the linkages between the stages and steps of the M&A process (Weber, Y. 2003). For example, the model suggests that cultural differences should be analyzed in the early stages of planning unlike the post-merger stream of research and the practitioners who focus on the role of cultural differences after the deal has been signed. This analysis serves not only the post-merger integration stage, but also all the other pre-merger stages, such as screening, financial and strategic evaluation, negotiation, final payment, and agreement details. Similarly, synergy analysis serves all other stages, and feedback from the negotiation stage serves the reassessment of cultural and synergy factors, and are used as inputs for such planning steps as screening, integration planning, and financial and strategy evaluations. The stages described here are amplified in subsequent chapters of the book, as you delve into depths and details of each issue.

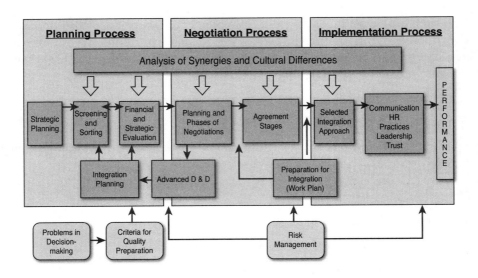

Figure 2.1   Model of Value Creation in M&A

Stage I: Planning and Strategic Management

1. Strategic Management, Goals, and M&A Strategy

In contrast to the "intuitive" approach followed by managers and owners in response to an M&A opportunity, the proactive approach proposed here is based on strategic planning for the company. In this planning process, management sets its financial and strategic goals, sets the strategic alternatives, and clarifies the ways in which the M&A strategy can assist in attaining both financial and strategic goals. Thus, the needs and advantages of the M&A are defined in advance of such strategic objectives as extending or adding products, services, and technologies, entering new geographical markets, entering into sources of supply or distribution (vertical integration) or entering a new line of business. For example, the company specifies which departments and products are those that can benefit more from M&A than from other growth and competitive strategies. It also considers other strategic alternatives to achieve its goals such as joint ventures or other strategic alliances. These considerations account for the financial goals such as improving revenues, EBITDA, cash flows, or other goals.

Every organization has limited resources and must decide on their distribution and allocation. Thus, the goals and strategy serve as the basis of the criteria for selecting a company for a merger and are the foundation of an M&A plan, for example, setting the goals of the acquisition (increasing market share, improving competitive advantages, acquiring new competitive abilities, entering a new industry, establishing a foothold in the international market, and so on), characterizing the target company (size, technology, competitive abilities, and domain), and specific type of possible acquisitions (supplier, client, competitor, and vendor of complementary products).

2. Searching, Screening, and Selection

Usually, every organization has several alternatives for an M&A, although management might not be aware of those. After management decides on its strategic goals and strategy to achieve these goals, the next step is to articulate an M&A plan. This plan helps to set criteria for searching candidates, for a thorough comparative system to screen candidates, and the selection of best alternatives for M&A. Thus, based on a viable corporate strategic plan, the M&A strategy delineates key objectives for the takeover that support the strategic goals and take into account resource constraints.

It is essential to consider strategic alternatives even if management thinks that it found the best target for acquisition. Alternatives help in negotiation because they can give a good estimation for the value of the target company and for other important issues not related directly to the price.

Again, in contrast to the intuitive approach, the M&A strategy and its planning process identify the various alternatives and ranks them. The criteria can be, for instance, the level of synergy in each merger, the obstacles to seize this synergy (for instance, due to cultural differences), the difficulty to integrate the two organizations, knowledge transfer, and of course financial value and the cost of acquisition. Therefore, screening and ranking are affected not only by strategic goals, which are the focus of practitioners in the early stages of the merger, but also by the integration planning process and by implementation challenges.

3. Financial and Strategic Estimate, Including Synergy Analysis and Corporate Culture Differences

In the intuitive approach, management requests a financial estimate of the value of the target company. By contrast, the proposed model emphasizes the importance of obtaining a strategic estimate in addition to a financial one. A strategic estimate takes into account the synergy potential of the merger, its contribution to the company's business strategy and predefined strategic goals, the method of implementing the merger by planning the subsequent integration of the organizations, and more. Such an estimate is crucial for the screening and ranking process. In some cases, the overall price is higher than suggested by the financial estimate, the premium price being justified by the strategic estimate. The opposite is also possible and the negotiation process results in a lower price than suggested by the financial estimate, but the strategic estimate and implementation challenges revealed during integration planning suggest foregoing this merger alternative.

4. Integration Planning

The integration planning and transition process begins usually after the agreement has been signed. According to the proposed model, this is too late. The aim of the integration of the two organizations is to exploit synergy. The decision maker must estimate the challenges and costs associated with the integration after planning and before the deal is signed. This information should be part of the negotiation process and affect the decision whether to acquire the target company, and if yes, affect many parts of the agreement, such as price and payments.

The stages of the post-agreement integration process and the implementation challenges in exploiting the synergy potential should be clear during the planning stages preceding the agreement. For example, decision makers should plan and consider the new structure of the organization as well as methods for overcoming corporate culture differences, maintaining human capital, addressing manager and employee stress and negative attitudes toward the merger, and identifying specific areas of synergy, cost-cutting, and knowledge transfer. If the difficulties, uncertainties, and costs of integration seem to be too high, the M&A should be declined. In sum, early planning of the integration affects the strategic and financial estimate, the negotiation process, as well as the screening and ranking of potential candidates for M&A.

Stage II: Negotiation, Due Diligence, and Agreement

1. The Negotiation Processes

Negotiations in M&A have unique characteristics not present in other negotiations. Israel Makov, former CEO of Teva, which pursued numerous M&As and became the largest generic pharmaceutical company in the world, maintained that one must "establish framework and guidelines for the negotiation (Forbes M&A conference 2007)."

There are different alternatives for approaching the target company, each of which has its advantages and disadvantages. First, focus on preliminary discussions and the creation of trust, personal "chemistry," and a mutual basis for creating value on both sides. Analysis of cultural differences, for instance, can help in the negotiation stage. Information on cultural differences, derived from the analysis at the planning stage, is useful in approaching the other company to explain together the advantages of the merger. There are numerous studies that confirm that deals have fallen through because the cultures of the two companies were vastly different. When the proposed merger between Monsanto and American Home Products (AHP) was called off in 1998, for example, the failure to reach an agreement was attributed to conflicting management styles. *The Wall Street Journal* article concluded, "Another drug industry mega-merger goes bust: Clash of cultures kills Monsanto-AHP marriage." A recent study shows that those who invest more in planning their negotiation and include cultural differences consideration were more successful in their deals.

The next step provides details on the writing of a Memorandum of Understandings (MOU) or Letter of Intentions (LOI), which marks an important change of style in the negotiation. Finally, the planning of the operation and integration of the two organizations is ideally carried out before the agreement. Thus, important stages of the implementation should be discussed before signing the deal, making possible a better understanding of the true potential of the rest of the synergic advantages and predicted obstacles, and a better understanding of differences in management styles and cultural differences. In addition, the knowledge accumulated in the negotiation serves as input for the re-evaluation of the earlier financial and strategic estimates and of the cost of the deal.

2. Assessment of Due Diligence

The process of inspecting the acquired company must be thorough and extensive to confirm assumptions made in the evaluation process, identify sources for the company's value, and minimize surprises after signing the agreement. Generally, the due diligence includes examinations in the accountancy and legal fields, but these aren't sufficient. According to the journalistic description of the Creo-Scitex deal, the management of Creo was surprised to discover after signing the deal that in many product domains there was no investment in R&D for promoting technologies and products. It was likewise surprised by the many differences in corporate culture. According to Claude Dion, head of the Hay Group in France, 58 percent of business leaders confess that intangible assets are often forgotten in the due diligence process, resulting in insufficient focus on intangible issues such as human capital and cultural differences during post-merger integration, increasing the risk of poor acquisition performance (Forbes M&A conference, 2007). These and other issues should surface in an extensive due diligence covering all company functions and domains of activity, as well as in examination of the fields, the country in which the company operates, and its laws. Furthermore, an extensive inspection must thoroughly cover HR, including the talents and managerial abilities of top managers, and look into other important domains such as the composition of the board of directors and the image that the public, analysts, stockholders, clients, suppliers, and others have of the company. Finally, the inspection must examine the unique advantages of the merger and not only the advantages and disadvantages of the target company, and place emphasis on the synergy and other strategic advantages stemming from the merger.

Stage III: Integrating the Organizations

1. Approaches to Integration, Cultural Differences, and Human Capital Integration

The value of an M&A is created after the agreement is signed through the integration of the two companies. But what are the areas of the two organizations that should be integrated? What are the steps to be followed? How should cultural differences be treated? How much autonomy should be granted to the acquired managers?

Unlike the intuitive approach that treats all M&As as similar, the value creation approach requires analysis, evaluation, and decision based on the best integration approach for each M&A. For example, ECI, an international telecom company, was purchased during the 1990s by an American company that decided to grant its managers full independence. This merger failed. Following this experience, ECI granted no autonomy in the acquisition of Tadiran Communication, and the acquired managers were not involved in any important decisions. The engineers and managers of Tadiran were surprised to discover one morning that all the signs had been changed, cars had been painted, and the name Tadiran had been replaced by ECI. This merger didn't turn out well either. Could both approaches followed by ECI be wrong? It is possible that both approaches might work in other mergers, that is, it might have been beneficial to allow Tadiran to keep its independence, and detrimental in the case of the merger with the American company. This case exemplifies the suggestion of several scholars that experience in M&A does not necessarily lead to better performance because top management might apply incorrectly its experience to a new acquisition that is not similar to a previous one made by the same managers (Finklestein and Haleblain, 2002; King et al., 2004).

The integration of the organizations can be carried out at several levels of intensity and speed. The appropriate degree depends on the aims of the integration (the synergy potential) and on the extent to which the organizations can be integrated (the implementation of the synergy potential).

The selection of an integration approach dictates the measures and actions to be taken during the first period following the merger. Recently, Teva reported completing the integration of a Dutch company, which took 15 months. Considering the size of the integrated company, the process was a swift one. Indeed, the complexity and length of the integration process requires considerable planning (refer to Figure 2.1), and it is advisable to carry out most of the planning before signing the agreement—otherwise the integration takes a long time, the costs are high, and the merger might fail to reach its goals.

Integration planning should include such steps as:

- Determining the integration approach, transition management structure

- Communication strategy, modification of the organization's corporate culture

- The handling of consequences of differences in managerial and organizational cultures

- Detailed consideration of human capital and key people retention, including all human resources issues such as staffing, training, rewarding, benefits, promotion (more as described in Chapters 10 to 16)

2. Leadership and Integration Infrastructure

The merger integration requires a "champion" who has the primary responsibility for leading the entire integration process. One alternative is for the integration manager (the CEO in some mega-mergers) to lead the M&A process through all its stages, including transaction, transition, and integration. The leader, with the executive team (sometimes called steering committee or merger coordination council) leads through a coordinating body that, among other responsibilities, sets guidelines consistent with the strategic direction, oversees analyses and findings, makes investment decisions, and monitors the implementation of integration plans.

Orchestrating the entire integration process requires the establishment of an infrastructure for the transition stage. The design of this formal transitional structure includes the establishment of a task force with specific assignments for each area of possible integration, the selection of task force leaders, arrangement of the kickoff session that begins the planning, creation of effective communication and coordination among task forces, and the provision of staff support, as well as inside and outside consultants.

3. Stress and Tension

The variables suggested in the first chapter (refer to Figure 1.2) are critical to the implementation of post-merger integration. Cultural differences, whether national or corporate, removal of autonomy from acquired top managers, and uncertainty surrounding the drama of the M&A result in stress, tension, and negative attitudes toward cooperation and commitment, given the psychological contract developed in every M&A (Weber and Drori, 2001). Furthermore, without professional intervention, stress and negative attitudes result in lower cooperation of the acquired management and lower commitment to the success of the integration process. Lower commitment, in turn, leads to high turnover among the acquired top management and talent, especially in the first year after the merger, which eventually degrades the financial performance of the merger.

4. Communication Strategy

Effective communication is essential for coping with the behavioral problems previously described. Well-informed employees and managers can keep more of their attention on the job at hand. Without systematic communication, uncertainty prevails and rumors become the main source of information. Uncertainty and poor communication strategy result in lost trust in management, morale and productivity problems, and the defection of key talent and customers—all detrimental to the integration process and the success of the merger.

The subjects, media, target audiences, goals, and processes of communication change over the different stages of the merger as the stakeholders change. An organized communication plan therefore must be prepared taking into account cultural differences, the type of synergy, the type of merger, and the partner. This plan ensures that the right communications are provided through the right channels to the right stakeholders at the right time. For instance, it was because of the lack of such a program that the merger of Deutsche Bank and Drezner Bank has not come about. The manager of Deutsche Bank, Rolf Breuer, was not clear enough about the advantages of the deal and about the future activities of the merged banks in the domain of investment banking. Consequently, investors on both sides refused to close a deal that could have launched a strong world power in the banking industry.

An effective communication plan for a merger is guided by several principles and a communication philosophy that represent the core values driving the plan. The execution of the plan must ensure that all communications are coordinated and consistent across different media channels and over time.

5. Cultural Assessment and Cultural Integration

Although cultural fit is known to be a major factor in the success of post-merger integration, cultural differences and their effects on the success of the merger are not always an essential part of every step of the M&A decision making. These steps include the negotiation of the deal price, systematic search, screening, sorting of candidates for acquisition, due diligence, the planning of post-merger integration that take place before the agreement, retaining key talent and top managers, and so on. For example, the top managers of Daimler declared in many instances that cultural differences were important in the acquisition of Chrysler, but most of the time, a discussion of cultural differences and the HR person were not included in the committee reporting to the CEO. In the proposed model, cultural differences play a major role at each important step in the management of the M&A.

The assessment of cultural fit is highly complex, in part because of problems in contact with the target firm and access to information about it. Various methods and processes are available for collecting data on cultural differences, using primary sources of information (that is, direct contact with the target company), such as questionnaires and interviews, and describing secondary sources of information (involving little or no contact with the target company) such as content analysis of articles and publications in newspapers and the Internet, target mission statements, target newsletters, speeches delivered by top managers, and more.

Finally, after creating an operational description of the cultures that form the mosaic of interrelated elements and processes, it becomes possible to actively manage the cultural integration of the merged company by means of training and development, reward systems, communication, correct leadership behavior, ceremonies and events, and so on.

6. Integration Approaches

All value creation in the M&A hinges on the combined firms' ability to effectively integrate their operations to exploit their potential synergy. The integration might adversely affect commitment of the acquired top management to cooperation with the acquiring management teams. Thus, there is an explicit trade-off between high and low levels of integration. High levels of integration might be needed to exploit high levels of synergy, but a high level of integration might cause HR problems that can destroy the value of the acquired firm and increase costs to an extent that offsets the benefits expected from the merger. This might explain the conflicting empirical findings about the relationships between integration and merger performance (Schweiger and Goulet, 2000; Weber et al., 2001).

Integration approaches differ mainly in the emphasis placed on two critical factors: synergy potential and implementation efforts necessary to realize potential synergies. Several matrices and descriptions suggest different integration approaches (Haspeslagh and Jemison, 1991; Schweiger, 2002; Ellis and Lamont, 2004), but they ignore or pay little attention to cultural differences between the two firms and are silent about the degree of integration within each approach and about its relationship with performance. Finally, the specific corporate and national cultural characteristics of the acquirer are not considered despite evidence suggesting that those characteristics are important elements in the integration decisions of the acquirer. In other words, the cultural *dimensions* of the acquirer affect its choice of level of integration, and eventually merger success.

Now consider a new three-dimensional framework for choosing integration approaches. The dimensions are

- Potential synergy in the M&A

- Corporate and national cultural differences between the two firms

- The corporate and national culture dimensions and characteristics of the acquirer

Unlike other matrices that merely suggest an integration approach, this three-dimensional framework is new in its practical guidance in the degree of integration *within* each approach and elaborating on the different managerial practices associated with each approach.

Furthermore, practical steps include implementing these approaches, considering such issues as which strategic capabilities need to be preserved, to what extent these capabilities depend on maintaining a cultural difference, and to what extent some capabilities need to be transferred.

7. Evaluation, Control, and Feedback

Two essential reasons exist for using a formal program to track the progress of such a complex combination. First, during the M&A, several mechanism processes can influence performance, and many steps can face problems during implementation. The complexity of the many activities to be managed during the process and the many unanticipated events can easily throw the process off track. Systematic and continuous assessment and improvement are key elements in the success of the M&A. Second, M&As are heterogeneous and inherently causally ambiguous. Therefore, much effort is needed to develop and update acquisition-specific methods, procedures, and systems that lower the degree of causal ambiguity among decisions, actions, and performance. Systematic track records are essential for the post-mortem process that can enhance the learning process of merger managers.

Methods, measures, and templates for control and evaluation in four areas must be defined in advance: operational measures, integration measures, cultural change measures, and naturally, financial performance. These measures and indexes make it possible for managers to examine the planned progress and make the required modifications when performance is not up to the defined standards.

Conclusion

Managing M&As is a complex process that requires a systematic approach that integrates knowledge accumulated in various disciplines. A multidisciplinary approach to value creation in M&As implies linkages between all stages of the process to achieve the ultimate goal of the M&As: the delivery of the expected financial results.

References

Chatterjee, S., Lubatkin, M. H., Schweiger, D. M., and Weber, Y. (1992). "Cultural differences and shareholder value in related mergers: Linking equity and human capital." *Strategic Management Journal*, 13, 319–334.

Ellis, K.M. and Lamont, B.T. (2004). "'Ideal' acquisition integration approaches in related acquisitions of equals: A test of long-held beliefs." *Advances in Mergers and Acquisitions*, 3, 81–102.

Finkelstein, S. and Haleblian, J. (2002). "Understanding acquisition performance: The role of transfer effects." *Organization Science*, 13, 36–47.

Forbes M&A conference, Tel Aviv, Israel, October 15, 2007.

Haspeslagh, P. and Jemison, D. B. (1991). *"Managing acquisitions and creating value through corporate renewal."* New York: Free Press.

King, D. R., Dalton, D. R., Daily, C. M., and Covin, J. G. (2004). "Meta-analyses of post-acquisition performance: Indications of unidentified moderators." *Strategic Management Journal*, 25,187–200.

Schweiger, M. D. (2002). "M&A integration: A framework for executives and managers." New York, NY/London, England: McGraw-Hill.

Schweiger, M. D. and Goulet, P. K. (2000). "Integrating mergers and acquisitions: An international research review." *Advances in Mergers and Acquisitions*, 1, 61–91.

Stahl, G. K., and Voigt, A. (2008). "Do cultural differences matter in mergers and acquisitions? A tentative model and examination." *Organization Science*, 19, 160–176.

Weber, Y. (2003). *Mergers and acquisitions management*. Peles:Rishon LeTzion (In Hebrew).

Weber, Y., Shenkar, O. and Raveh, A. (1996). "National and corporate cultural fit in mergers/acquisitions: An exploratory study." *Management Science*, 42(8), 1215–1227.

Weber, Y. and Drori, I. (2011). "Integration of organizational and human behavior perspectives on mergers and acquisitions: Looking inside the black box." *International Studies of Management and Organization*, 41(3), 76–95.

Weber, Y. and Fried, Y. (2011a). "The role of HR practices in managing culture clash during the post-merger integration process." *Human Resource Management*, 50(5), 565–570.

Weber, Y. and Fried, Y. (2011b). "The dynamic of employees' reactions during post-merger integration process." *Human Resource Management*, 50(6), 777–781.

Weber, Y. and Tarba, S.Y. (2011). "Exploring culture clash in related merger: Post-merger integration in the hightech industry." *International Journal of Organizational Analysis*, 19(3), 202–221.

Weber, Y., Tarba, S. Y., and Reichel, A. (2011). "International mergers and acquisitions performance: Acquirer nationality and integration approaches." *International Studies of Management & Organization*, 41(3), 9–24.

3

STRATEGIC MOTIVES AND CONSIDERATIONS

Introduction

The main theme of this book is that successful M&As are based on systematic management of a strategic decision-making process and the outcome actions. This is in contrast to the *intuitive* approach in which management captures sporadic opportunities but fails to achieve its goals. Contrary to what many executives might think, the approach here is that M&As are not strategies in and of themselves, but rather part of the corporate strategic implementation stage. This book suggests a different approach that focuses on M&A strategy as part of overall corporate and competitive strategies rather than focusing on the specific acquisition solely. Thus, this chapter opens with a description of the motives for M&A and thereafter articulates the strategic management process that includes M&As.

Strategic Motives for an M&A

There are numerous motives and related theories that explain why an M&A takes place. One common approach suggests that the main motive of the M&A is value creation for stakeholders. A main motive here is the attempt to seize potential synergy from the M&A in which the value of the combined firms is greater than the sum of the values of each firm. In this approach, managers are expected to maximize shareholders' interests and create value from a rational estimation of the accurate potential of the M&A to create such value.

Another approach assumes that many managers focus on their own individual motives rather than the shareholders' interests. According to this cynical approach, often attributed to economics scholars who expect a high premium to be paid for the target company, senior managers engaged in M&A might or might not create value to stakeholders. Pursuing M&A strategy can promote their own "empire-building" efforts driven by desire to lead larger organizations, improve their relative standing and status in the industry, and satisfies their own ego.

The *industry motives* are based on changes that drive organizations to merge such as globalizations, or industry consolidations that increase market power of competitors or create threats of limited access to supply or distribution channels. It should be indicated that responses to some of those threats are often termed as a *vertical integration merger*. Specifically, mergers due to threats such as constrain on supply or limited access to customers might not create value but are essential to organizational survival.

The *organizational motives* might include such issues as value creation via the opportunity to seize various synergies in the M&A such as cost synergy, knowledge transfer in various functions, or general management synergy. Other reasons for the M&A might include improving competitive position, accessing new markets, and the decision to "buy" technology or knowledge rather than develop it internally.

Finally, the i*ndividual motives* might include personal reasons of top executives that were mentioned earlier. In addition to those motives, managers have the opportunity to get better rewards and compensations due to the increased responsibilities of managing larger organizations. And in some cases, top executives of both buying and target companies might get a large bonus just to accomplish a merger, such as in the case of the HP and Compaq merger.

This book focuses on *value creation motives*. These include strategic and financial motives. Moreover, as was explained in Chapter 2, "An Integrated Model for Value Creation in Mergers and Acquisitions," the focus is on the relationships between such strategic and financial motives for all stages of the merger including the post-merger integration process. Therefore, more on the merger motives is discussed later in this chapter.

Synergy

Pursuing synergy is one of the main reasons mentioned to explain M&A activity. The main idea is that the combination of two companies can create value to shareholders than if these two businesses operate separately. Chapter 5, "Synergy Potential and Realization," articulates the various components of synergy and managerial tools that analyze and assess the achievement of synergy.

Often elusive, when managed well, firms can gain benefits from seizing synergy in M&A activity. It can create additional value by the combination of existing resources of both companies. For example, the achievement of lower average costs (and thereby higher profits) is one of the main motives for the M&A. Through cooperation, firms can achieve economies through rationalization of various functions and units of the organization, such as the production process, leading to reductions in cost per unit as output increases and companies share costs. Synergy can be achieved through economies of scale by spreading of fixed costs, such as infrastructure and headquarter costs, and over-increasing production levels combined from the two companies.

The M&A can also achieve economies of scope. The concept of scope economies refers to the abilities of a diversified firm to share investments and costs across different value chains, such as costs of joint development, production, marketing, or distribution of various products. Thus, synergy can also be achieved by increasing revenues without increasing the combined costs of the two businesses in the M&A, for instance, by cross-selling products through complementary sales organizations and distribution channels.

Market Power

The acquisition of a competitor increases the market power of the buyer company. It allows the buyer to maintain or increase prices of services or products, thereby improving margins. Thus, the elimination of competitors and capacity from the market is a main motive of the M&A.

Three situations usually induce the M&A aimed at increasing market power:

- A fall in demand results in excess capacity and hence a threat of price-cutting competition. In this situation, the M&A secures a better competitive position that allows maintaining, or increasing, prices.
- Low barriers to entry and the prospects of international competition threaten an overcapacity and price decrease.
- Tightening of legislation might make some types of alliances between companies illegal; then the M&A becomes a good alternative.

Therefore, via the M&A, competitors and capacity could be taken out of the market and the results are increased market power, prices, and margins for the remaining players.

Diversification

The objective of diversification is to buy firms outside of the buyer's core businesses and markets. Diversification takes place when a firm enters new markets and industries in which the buyer has little or no previous experience. Thus, the firm can diversify its activities and hope to grow revenues by adding new products and services, acquiring new technologies rather than trying to develop with its current resources, and acquiring new management talents.

However, consistent findings show that diversification in many cases reduced shareholders' values, and it proved easier for investors to diversify their own personal portfolios than for firms to do so. (Few exceptions exist, such as Berkshire Hathaway.) Top managers justify such M&As on the basis of reducing shareholder risk by spreading investments and assets in several industries and thereby reducing the dependency on one or few sources of revenue. A main reason for diversification was the desire to find businesses with uncorrelated cash flows, so the combined cash flow might be less volatile to unexpected surprises in core products and industries. The main analogy was that a corporation might be more stable if it has more legs.

Another common motive for diversification is to shift assets from current core business in which their growth rate has decreased or is expected to decrease into other markets and industries that have higher growth potential. The M&A alternatives seem to be better for those corporations than trying to follow internal growth by developing their own product or market. A famous example is the purchase of AMC by Chrysler because of the Jeep, rather than developing it by itself and SUV due to the expectation of a relatively long time to market factor that may allow competitors to catch the main volume of that market.

Financial and Tax Issues

Unlike synergy from operations, there are potential benefits of the cost of capital of the buying firm or the newly formed firm resulting from the M&A. Although reduction in cost of capital might result from operation synergy, there are other sources such as from lower securities and transactions costs. For example, larger firms might issue debt at a lower average interest rate and also lower costs of legal fees or common equity. There might also be opportunities for tax savings, such as a carryover of net losses, an increase in leverage, and a change in the tax basis in asset depreciation.

Valuation Ratio

The valuation ratio (market value/asset value) might be a motive for the M&A. First, top management of a corporation might have general management skills, such as abilities to formulate and implement appropriate competitive strategies, that might be transferred to the new acquired company and improve its performance. There are corporations that buy companies relatively cheaply on the stock exchange and sell them later after performance improvement or sell parts of them off at a profit later. Another reason might be associated with imperfections in capital markets, if a company is "undervalued" because its share price is low compared to the value of its assets, and then it becomes vulnerable to a takeover. Usually it can happen when a firm has a low payout ratio to retain a high proportion of profits for reinvestment. Another possibility for discrepancies in asset valuations is even higher in cases involving firms from different countries.

Agency Theory

According to *agency theory*, the main objective of managers is growth of the firm, rather than its profitability. Because the majority of companies involved in this type of activity are run by employed managers rather than its shareholders, managers might, therefore, be more interested in raising their power, status, salaries, and job security through the growth of the firm.

Agency theory suggests that fast-growing firms, having already adopted a growth-maximization approach, are the ones most likely to be involved in the M&A. These theories also suggest that fast-growing firms give higher remuneration to managers and raise job security by being less prone to takeover. Some scholars argue that despite the fact that there is not a correlation between the size of the firm and its profitability, large firms are less likely to be taken over than small- to medium-sized firms (Gomes, E., Angwin, D., Weber, Y., and Tarba, S.Y. 2013). They state that any given percentage increase in size was much more significant in reducing the probability of a takeover for the large firm than it was for the small- to medium-sized firm. Therefore, firms might have a comprehensive tendency to become larger to build defenses against possible takeovers.

The Strategic Management of M&As as Part of Corporate and Competitive Strategies

To decide on an M&A and execute successfully, this strategic direction must be driven by a sound corporate and business strategy. Yet, too many times, management makes its strategic choices by reacting to emergent threats or opportunities without having an overall strategic plan for growth. The purpose of this section is to offer a planning-based approach to M&As that is part of the overall strategy of an organization.

Although some suggest that strategy is basically a way of thinking and others suggest focusing on flexibility and strategic agility, those approaches, although appealing given day-to-day challenges, are difficult to apply in practice because they provide little guidance for their implementation. A systematic planning approach has its merits as does any strategic planning, not only as knowledge creation in current and future situations, but also as preparation to unexpected situations, involvement and motivation of those managers who will implement the M&A, creation of control systems, and more.

One of the major roles of top executives is to identify markets and industries in which their company should compete, and how it should compete, to maximize its long-term growth and profitability. For this aim, top executives engage in a strategic management process to decide the overall strategy. There are two essential decisions for the M&A. The first is *if and when to use the M&A as part of the overall strategy*. There are many strategic options to achieve growth and profitability, such as joint ventures, outsourcing, and investments in product and company differentiation; entering international markets via contracts with franchisee; developing new products, and more. In all cases, the M&A can be an alternative, such as in the last example for the development of a new product, management might decide to "make" or "buy," namely to acquire a company with the product or technology.

Small scale entails relatively fewer investments and a smaller amount of cash flow over time and for a shorter period of time, and thus, less risk. However, the expected profit and cash flow are relatively lower (see Figure 3.1).

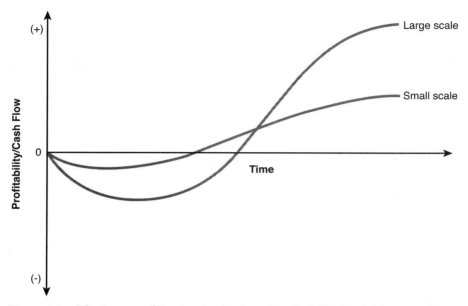

Figure 3.1   The Impact of Production Scale on Profitability/Cash Flow over Time

If the answer to the first decision is positive and management decides to acquire a company, the second strategic decision is *to choose the best target company to acquire* In most cases, the best target company for acquisition is chosen from a list of potential companies that will be analyzed and considered for acquisitions. The strategic management model (see Figure 3.2) enables systematic analyses and responses to each of the previous two decisions. Furthermore, it enables analyzing candidates for the M&A and evaluating the fit between the two organizations. Later, in Chapter 7, "Screening and Selection of M&A Alternatives," a more elaborated process is presented. Finally, with this model, the top executives can do the first step that appears in the Value Creation Model for the M&A that was presented in Chapter 2, "An Integrated Model for Value Creation in Mergers and Acquisitions."

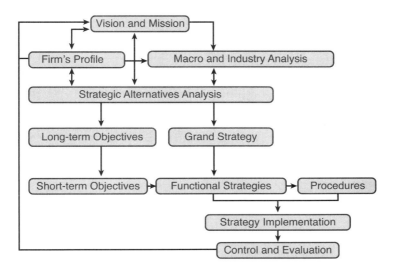

Figure 3.2   Strategic Management Model

The two most important decisions that any top executive team faces are the long-term goals (measurable) and the choice of a Grand Strategy that will be implemented to achieve the long-term goals. This Grand Strategy guides all actions in all units.

To make these two essential decisions for the future growth and profitability of the firm, data will be collected and analyzed. The data will be about the opportunities and threats in the organization's environment and its industry, as well as about the competitive advantages and disadvantages, strengths and weaknesses, and its tangible and intangible resources. This analysis will bring up the strategic alternatives that the firm faces and the challenging, but reasonable, long-term goals.

The chosen Grand Strategy and long-term goals guide the implementation plan that must fit the strategy and goals. It should be noted that the choice of Grand Strategy and goals also depends on the feasibility of the implementation process. As part of the implementation plan, short-term goals and functional strategies for each function such as marketing, human resources, finance, logistics, and so on will be determined and derived from the Grand Strategy and goals.

Similarly, the implementation plan provides changes in the organization's structure and organizational culture; both have to fit the Grand Strategy and long-term goals. Finally, a control and evaluation system will be established to fit all processes, stages, and decision making about all parts of the organization and the strategic management model. Figure 3.3 illustrates the relationships between the variables of the strategic implementation plan.

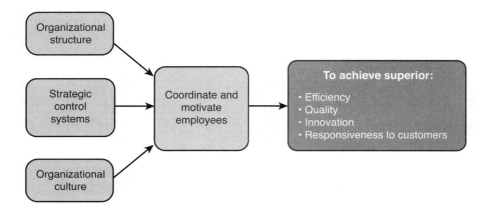

Figure 3.3   Strategic Implementation Plan

This strategic management model can guide two main decisions about the M&A. One refers to the use of the M&A as strategy, and the second refers to the choice of the partner. These two decisions are discussed in the next chapter.

One decision is about using the M&A as part of the strategy management process to achieve long-term growth and profitability. The second decision refers to the choice of the appropriate firm for the M&A that provides the best strategic fit between the two firms in the combination. The next chapter describes in a systematic way and in more details the decision-making processes for these two major strategic decisions about M&A.

References

Gomes, E., Angwin, D., Weber, Y., and Tarba, S.Y. (2013). Critical success factors through the mergers and acquisitions process: Revealing pre- and post-M&A connections for improved performance. *Thunderbird International Business Review*, 55 (1), 13-35.

4

M&A STRATEGIC DECISIONS

The previous chapter provides a systematic process to make M&A strategic decisions. This chapter presxents in detail this decision-making process and explain the two main M&A strategic decisions. One decision is about using M&A as part of the strategy management process to achieve long-term growth and profitability. The second decision refers to the choice of the appropriate firm for M&A that provides the best strategic fit between the two firms in the combination. Here are more details about these two decisions.

Decision 1: Should the M&A be Part of the Current Strategy?

Many organizations make their strategic decisions and choices by reacting to emergent needs, threats, or opportunities without having an overall consistent strategy for growth. For example, a company that was not planning on any M&A activity might be approached to assess its interest in a particular M&A, but having a planned strategy is certainly the preferred approach. Whenever possible, the decision to acquire or merge should be the outcome of a continuous strategic process rather than just a last minute knee-jerk reaction.

To adequately assess whether an M&A is an appropriate strategy for the firm, there is a need for a clear view of the firm's strategic context. By having a defined strategy for growth, firms can have more options for strategic directions, and thus, can clearly assess if the M&A is preferable to other strategic alternatives, as well as a clear vision of the type of M&A that fits its strategy and goals.

Many firms have a merger budget whereby managers are encouraged to seek out potential strategic targets, and then they are evaluated on the performance of the merger. Yet, the decision to use the M&A as a path for growth, although popular, should be made only after using a strategic management process like suggested earlier in

Chapter 3. For example, using the strategic management model, it is necessary that companies undertake a thorough analysis of the industry and external environment before making any major strategic choice in terms of M&A activity. Similarly, it is critical to assess if the contextual, political, social, and economic climates are conducive to the formation of partnerships. For instance, is the local government receptive to the concept of private sector participation? How are the relationships between the local government, the communities, and the private sector? How does the regulatory environment relate to market consolidation? These and other aspects of the macro environment must be carefully assessed.

Equally important is an analysis of the industry and the competitive environment to find out what is the degree of rivalry within an industry? How does it affect its attractiveness in terms of potential for profit? Which are the critical success factors of an industry and its associated markets? These and other aspects of the micro environment should be analyzed using frameworks such as Porter's Five Forces, life cycle analysis, strategic group analysis, market segmentation, and so on, as shown in Figure 4.1.

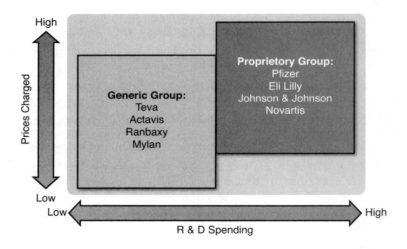

Figure 4.1   Strategic Groups in Pharmaceutical Industry

The final analysis should include all the opportunities and threats posed to organizations. Based on a thorough assessment of all these factors, organizations will be much better positioned to achieve their organizational purposes by making better strategic choices in terms of collaborative arrangements.

In the same way, an analysis of the internal capabilities of the company is also necessary. For this purpose, an analysis of the value chain of the organization is important. The value-chain concept distinguishes between primary and support activities (see Figure 4.2).

Therefore, it is necessary to undertake an analysis of the resources that are deployed into these activities, the linkages between them, and the competencies involved in the process of value creation. This can enable organizations to evaluate their core competencies and real strategic capabilities, upon which they can achieve a competitive advantage in providing more value for customers than other competitors.

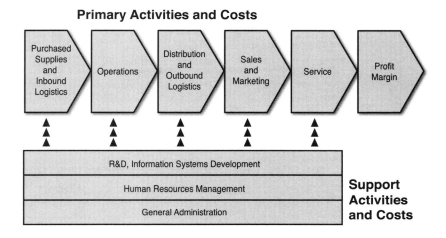

Figure 4.2   The Firm's Value Chain Model

When the firm realizes it needs to improve or acquire a number of resources or competencies to operate more adequately some of the activities of its value chain, then it might decide to do it internally (MAKE) or externally by the M&A (BUY). When firms have different core competencies and contribute to different value-chain activities, they might form a complementary strategic alliance or joint venture or buy these resources and competencies.

Another important consideration is the stakeholder expectations and organizational purposes. This is the case because the wants and needs of individuals and various groups, with interest and influence on the firm, are key elements of the strategic management process. Whatever the power structure on the process of strategic choice, their role in the implementation process will be critical. Therefore, it is strongly recommended that a thorough analysis of the various stakeholders' expectations and their involvement in the process be conducted. Figure 4.3 gives an example about the group of customers.

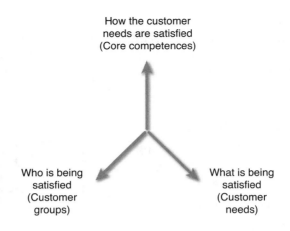

Figure 4.3   Definition of the Firm's Mission Model

Customer groups and needs and the related distinctive competencies might influence the choice of the M&A or an alternative strategy to achieve important competencies along the value-chain activities. This might influence the business definition that is an essential part of the mission and vision of the firm. A revision of the mission statement might be recommended for strategic decisions about the scope of investments in the M&A, for instance, to enter new markets, regions, or industries.

Decision 2: Choice of the Appropriate Partner for the M&A: Strategic Fit and Post-Merger Integration (PMI)

A successful M&A begins with self-scrutiny and analyses that yield a conclusion that a firm can realize strategic goals more realistically, rapidly, and/or cost-efficiently through the M&A than by acting on its own. The strategic management model and its components serve to examine every candidate firm for the M&A. With this model, it is possible to examine the strategic and organizational fit between one's company and the partner for the merger. There are three main issues to address:

1. Potential synergy

2. The ability to seize the potential synergy

3. The risk, costs, and length of the implementation of the merger, namely, the PMI process and its challenges

The components of the upper part of the strategic management model can serve as a guide for the analysis of the synergy potential. The mission statement and business definition (refer to Figure 4.3) of the two companies will be examined to see the similarities and differences between them. Some differences can enrich both companies. However, big differences on how the two top management teams see their businesses might cause major conflicts. Similarly, the companies' profiles will be analyzed and compared to find resources and skills that can be shared or transferred from one organization to the other. Some of the resources and skills will be complementary resources, whereas others will be similar. The analysis of what should be transferred, where to cut costs due to redundancy, how to transfer, and so on need a systematic process.

The components of the lower part of the strategic management model can serve for the analysis of the ability to seize the potential synergy. Thus, the strategy implementation part, especially systematic analysis of both organizational and national cultural differences, can give a good idea about the challenges in achieving synergy for a particular M&A. The systematic analysis, methods, main cultural dimensions, and use in all M&A stages are described in Chapter 5, "Synergy Potential and Realization."

The integration process and its challenges need to be analyzed *before* making a choice during the planning process that includes screening of candidates. This integration process needs to take into account cultural differences and potential clashes, potential lower commitment and cooperation of acquired managers, and turnover of acquired top executives and key talents at the first year after the merger. These issues are described in several chapters in Part IV, "Post-Merger Integration and Implementation." The process of screening and the managerial tool are discussed in Chapter 6, "Culture and Cultural Differences Analysis."

Diversification: Two Main Types of M&As

Diversification is the process of entering new industries that are different from a firm's core industry. This means that the firm will sell new products to customers in new markets that are distinct from the company's original market. This requires several considerations that are elaborated in the next section.

Entering into a New Industry

To succeed in entering into other industries, three tests must be met:

- **Potential for profit in the industry**—The chosen industry needs to be sufficiently profitable so that it is worthwhile considering it as opposed to other industries.

- **Costs of entry into the industry**—The entrance into the industry entails overcoming the entry barriers, and there might be sharp responses on the part of the competitors to the point that future profits are eliminated.

- **Synergetic advantages**—The new unit is supposed to give to the corporation or receive from it further advantages that will provide profit beyond the costs of the acquisition or the establishment of the new unit and beyond the costs of penetrating into the industry.

A firm that diversifies to a new industry usually has little or no previous experience in it. Acquiring a company in this industry is also an acquisition of knowledge about operating and competing in the new environment. Such acquisition is usually a high level of investment versus entering the new industry through internal new venturing. In other words, acquisition is a high-scale entrance, with the risk of having to deal with cultural differences and integration process challenges. In contrast, in internal new venturing, the investments usually are smaller and take a longer time, but lack knowledge about the industry. Here is a summary of some advantages and disadvantages of entrance by acquisitions:

- Competencies important in a new business area are lacking for the buying firm.
- Speed of entry is important.
- Acquisition is perceived as a less risky form of entry.
- Barriers to entry can be overcome by acquisition.

Acquisition as a mode of entry to a new industry might have the following disadvantages:

- Failing to follow through PMI of the acquired firm
- Overestimating the economic benefits of the acquisition
- Underestimating the costs involved in an acquisition
- Failing to properly screen candidates and find the appropriate acquisition

Another type of consideration for firms is about the two major ways to diversify their businesses in other industries so their long-term profitability will grow. These two types of diversification are unrelated diversification when they enter an industry that is different from their current business and related diversifications that include horizontal and vertical integration.

Unrelated Diversification: New Business

Unrelated diversification refers to a strategy in which the acquirer enters into a business with little or no previous experience. The objective is to diversify away from the firm's core business due to a small potential to keep the same growth rate as before, antitrust challenges, and/or reduce the risk of overdependence on one or few businesses or industries. A reduction in the firm's risks, for instance due to uncorrelated cashflow, can also reduce the cost of capital. Some companies such as Tyco, Berkshire Hathaway, and General Electric were successful in pursing this strategy. But those are rare cases. Most conglomerates never delivered value to their shareholders.

It is easier for investors to diversify their personal investment portfolios than for companies to do so. Research has proven that it is a risky strategy because it requires moving into unknown product and market areas. A recent, exhaustive study (Palich, L., Cardinal, L., and Miller, C.C. 2000) synthesized findings from three decades of research on diversification-performance linkage and reached a conclusion that moderate levels of diversification yield higher levels of performance than either limited or extensive diversification (see Figure 4.4).

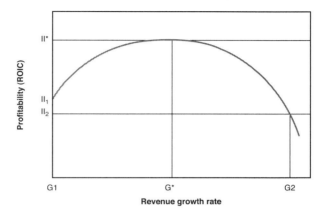

Figure 4.4   The Curvilinear Impact of Diversification on Firm's Performance

More specifically, their research provided corroborative evidence to the curvilinearity effect, namely, the performance increases as firms shift from single business strategies to related diversification, but performance decreases as firms change from related diversification to unrelated diversification. One of the reasons for lower levels of success is related to the fact that diversification necessarily causes the increase of the entire organization's expenses. These corporate costs (overhead and management resources) are allocated to every product or business unit. There are also managerial attention costs that distract the top key executives and talent from their main businesses, and this is detrimental to their performance. The management of every business unit dedicates time for reporting to the head management, for planning and coordination with other business units, and for corporate functions, such as human resources, advertisement, financing, and so on.

Related Diversification

Related diversification refers to a strategy in which the acquirer enters a new business that is related to its existing business units by some linkage between any parts of its value-chain functions and its new business. Related diversification aims to increase profit and sales from resource sharing or leveraging distinctive competencies and transferring know-how and skills from one company to the other. Thus, any best practices in any function such as marketing, manufacturing, and logistics can be transferred to improve competitive advantages of the buyer or the target company. This strategy focuses on the synergy potential between the two business units that merge. The main two M&A options are horizontal integration and vertical integration.

Horizontal Integration

This M&A strategy focuses on competition within a single market or industry. This allows managers to promote the organizational cohesiveness by using their knowledge and resources for competition in one area. These types of relationships are seen as a means to achieve lower cost structure through the exploitation of economies of scale and scope at the level both of the plant (productive unit) and the firm (business unit). Thus, the M&A achieves the benefits of lower fixed costs through the elimination of redundant units, departments, and functions. This type accounts for the majority of merger cases in various industries. For example, consider the merger between Daimler and Chrysler in the car industry, the Fuji-Xerox joint venture in the micro-film industry, the acquisition of P-Plus by SmarTone, and the minority investment of Deutsche Telekom in Islacom in the communications industry.

Horizontal M&As also aim to reduce industry rivalry by the elimination of a competitor, to increase market share and get higher prices through elimination of capacity from the marketplace. It is also an attempt by companies to gain control of business activity to increase the firm's dominance in its exchange relationships with other firms. It can also increase product differentiation by combining the product lines so that it can offer a wider range of products that can be bundled together. Thus, customers can buy a complete range of products at a single combined price and often obtain a price discount. A related way to increase product differentiation is through cross-selling. Here the M&A takes advantage of, or leverages, its established connections with customers by acquiring additional products or categories that it can sell to them. Providing a total solution saves customers time and money because they do not have to deal with various suppliers. Thus, horizontal integration increases the differentiated appeal and value of the merged companies' products.

The horizontal merger helps to increase competitive capabilities by acquiring new products, services, skills, knowledge, and technologies, as well as access to complementary distribution channels. Because creating and building a strong brand is something that normally takes a long period to develop, an acquisition can be the quickest and most effective means to buy an already established strong brand. This was precisely the case when the Indian car manufacturer Tata Motors and the Chinese car maker Nanjing/SAIC took over Jaguar/Land Rover and MG Motors, respectively. This assumption is supported by the market-power theory arguing that organizations can improve their competitive success by increasing their market power, which can also be achieved through collaboration with other organizations.

Horizontal mergers have also been employed by many consumer goods firms that have sought to round out their product offerings and by pharmaceutical firms that have attempted to improve their pipeline of new products.

Horizontal mergers also enable the merged company to obtain bargaining power over suppliers and buyers. This enables reduced costs of suppliers' products or increased prices to buyers.

Depending on the specific objectives of the companies involved and the situation of the industry in which they operate, the M&A can be enacted as an offensive or defensive move. The *offensive* move aims to develop firms' competitive advantages and to weaken other competitors' positions. In contrast, the *defensive* move is formed by organizations to build entry barriers to secure their competitive position and to defend themselves against a dominant player.

As discussed earlier, the M&A often fails to achieve the planned goals for several reasons, such as inability to deal with the challenges of cultural differences, high turnover of top managers, and key talents, as well as underestimating the problems of integration and poor planning of the PMI process and the tendency to overestimate the gains from the M&A. Other problems related to horizontal mergers are the overdependence on one industry and that large size brings the firm into conflict with the antitrust authorities.

Vertical Integration

Unlike horizontal mergers, the objective of vertical integrations is to enter into the sources of supply (backward vertical integration) and/or distribution channels (forward vertical integration). These can occur when firms combine at different stages of production of common goods or services, and it can happen backward and/or forward of its actual value chain to expand a firm's control over more aspects of the business for reasons of security of operation and to reduce dependency on other businesses. These moves require relatively low levels of organizational integration and standardization but high levels of coordination. Of course, a firm can decide to expand its operation without the M&A and enter a new industry. For example, Apple Computer entered the retail industry when it established a chain of Apple Stores to sell its iPods and computers.

Whatever choice is made, vertical integration lowers costs, increases product differentiation, or reduces industry competition when it facilitates investments in efficiency-enhancing assets and secure product quality, and results in improved scheduling. Some of these can be achieved by lower variable costs of raw materials, lower overall costs through improved product development and manufacturing interfaces, and minimized costs of managing the external relationships such as purchasing function.

If the vertical integration is *backward* toward the source of supply, firms might benefit by exerting closer control over quality and delivery of supplies, which might be cheaper after they can be obtained at a cost price. This might be exerted as a mechanism to reduce or eliminate dependence on any particular supplier. Examples for such moves are the acquisition of lighting, heating, and plumbing companies by Home Depot to have better control of the sources of supply.

When a firm is in an expanding phase, this can be a quicker and easier way to obtain a modern plant with special equipment rather than by doing it on its own. The same can be applied to cases in which firms want to acquire new technology, know-how derived from R&D competencies, or even patents.

When the vertical integration is *forward*, the firm can gain more control of wholesale or retail pricing policy and more direct customer contact. Thus, it can be an attempt to ensure a continuous demand for its products. Through such an M&A, the firm can acquire a marketing organization or simply gain access to new distribution channels; it can also enable the firm to enter new geographical areas. Vertical collaboration becomes ever-increasingly important because of several factors. This is because more and more of today's products require so many different technologies that most organizations can no longer maintain cutting-edge sophistication in all of them. This demands continuous collaboration between the organizations operating at the different stages of the value-creation process. Another important driver of this type of collaboration is that to compete globally, organizations have to share with partners the immense fixed costs of their complex and continuously growing operations.

Each stage of the value-added chain is a different industry in which there are many companies that can compete in those industries. Therefore, such M&As have to consider how much establishing operations at a stage in the value chain will compete with others versus increasing product differentiation or lower costs. Further, some companies, like the pulp and paper industry, achieve full vertical integration when they produce all the inputs needed for processes or dispose of all completed products through their own operations.

To sum up, major advantages of a vertical integration strategy:

- Builds entry barriers by requiring inputs and preserving existing loyal customers making them unavailable to new competitors
- Facilitates investments in efficiency-enhancing assets that solve planning and internal mutual dependence problems
- Improves planning and scheduling responses
- Protects product quality through control of input and distribution and service of outputs

Although vertical integration has many advantages, it can increase cost structure when its own in-house supplier lacks the incentive to reduce operating costs and loses competitive abilities due to safe selling to its own buyer. In such situations, other independent suppliers might supply the same inputs with lower costs to competitors. In cases of fast technological changes in the industry, a vertically integrated company might find itself locked into an old, inefficient technology that prevents it from changing to a new one. The following are some disadvantages of vertical integration:

- Cost of internal supply purchasing.

- Remaining with obsolescent technology.

- Aligning input and output capacities with uncertainty and fluctuations in market demand is difficult.

In such cases, the alternatives to vertical integration strategies are strategic alliances such as joint ventures that are the subject of the following section.

Joint Ventures

Many of the benefits associated with vertical integration can be achieved through strategic alliances with different types of long-term agreements about cooperative relationships with companies along the value-added chain. These cooperative agreements run the gamut from establishing formal joint ventures to short-term contractual agreements, for instance, the establishment of prices and conditions under which the raw material will be purchased.

Joint ventures are entities formed for a specific purpose in which two or more organizations have an equity stake in an independent business entity. Unlike most partnerships, the duration of a joint venture is predetermined anticipating the eventual termination of the agreement. Such joint ventures can involve two or more legally different organizations (the parents), each of which invest in the joint venture (the child) and actively participate in the decision-making activities of the jointly owned entity.

Joint ventures are one of the most preferred types of alliances with many advantages, especially as an entry mode to the international arena. A company might benefit from a foreign partner that has the knowledge of the host country's competitive conditions, political systems, culture, and language. For example, in some countries, the political regulations make joint ventures the only feasible entry mode. Thus, during the 1990s, joint ventures were widely used by Western companies as a means to get access to Eastern markets, such as Japan and China.

However, joint ventures have a high failure rate because often one of the partners tends to take a dominant role in the partnership. A joint venture can risk giving control of its technology to its partner. Another disadvantage is that joint ventures do not give tight control as M&As do. This can prevent the company from the realization of an experience-curve or location economies. Decision-making processes can be difficult due to the need to consider the partner in any process and investment. In the global arena, it can cause problems of engaging in global strategic coordination for the company that depends on the partner of the joint venture.

Strategic Outsourcing

Strategic outsourcing is a situation in which one company allows one or more of its value-chain activities or functions to be performed by another company. This can happen when the other company becomes a specialist and has skills and knowledge of a specific kind of activity of the chain. Outsourcing a value-chain activity allows the company to focus on less value-creation activities to strengthen its other activities. The value-chain partnership can take place when one organization forms a long-term collaboration agreement with a key supplier or distributor for a mutual advantage. An example is the lean production system introduced by Japanese car manufacturers, initially known as Toyotism, that is contrary to the old Fordist mass production system where there was a tendency for companies to integrate vertically as much as possible. With the lean production system, however, *collaboration* became the key word.

Outsourcing activities are usually those that managers regard as noncore or nonstrategic. Recognizing the need to focus on their core business, companies tend to outsource more and more activities that are not a source of the companies' distinctive competencies and competitive advantage over external suppliers specializing in those activities. Thus, instead of maintaining an arms-length short-term relationship with their suppliers and buyers, firms prefer to establish a long-term collaborative relationship with them.

This new pattern has altered the supply-chain management in various industries. As a result, companies of the same value system started to work more closely with fewer selected suppliers and to involve them more and more in the product design process. The advantages of strategic outsourcing include lower cost structure and enhanced differentiation, for instance, via quality improvements and more innovations. This consequently increased competitive positions for the collaborating partners. This resulted in a variety of collaborative arrangements through which companies cooperate at the various stages of their value chain, such as just-in-time supplier relationships, sole source suppliers, joint development, technology sharing and cross-licensing agreements, value-added remarketers and resellers, and value-added dealers.

Strategic outsourcing can have some risks such as losing a competitive advantage to a partner who might become a potential competitor. Furthermore, a company might become too dependent on the provider of the specific value-chain activity. Therefore, companies need to be open to sharing resources and competencies with partners without giving away their core competencies.

Reference

Palich, L., Cardinal, L., and Miller, C.C. (2000). Curvilinearity in the diversification-performance linkage. *Strategic Management Journal*, 21, 155–174.

PART II
Analysis Tools for Key Success Factors

5

SYNERGY POTENTIAL
AND REALIZATION

Introduction

Synergy potential is the primary reason voiced by managers who explain the rationale for the M&A that they are performing. However, the high percentage of failures of M&As indicates that the declared synergy in many mergers was either an illusion and was not appropriately identified, or the integration program was not properly implemented and therefore was not realized. This chapter describes the different areas of synergy and thus enables evaluation and focus of the management on the true potential of synergy. In addition, several sections elaborate on knowledge transfer as a growing source of synergy in M&As. Finally, this chapter proposes a method that facilitates the identification and analysis of synergy potential in mergers.

Sources of Synergies

The main incentive for an M&A is the added value creation for both parties as a result of a process used to generate synergies. In an M&A, the term *synergy* refers to a situation in which the sum of the parts, activities, and processes is more than their arithmetic value prior to becoming a combined entity. In a simpler way, the synergy in an M&A is a state in which two merged business entities have larger revenues and/or lower costs and, thus, higher profits.

There are several potential sources of added value creation in an M&A. These include three main areas that require good managerial skills for realization of synergies:

- Shared resources such as activities and facilities

- Transfer of functional knowledge and capabilities between the two firms
- Transfer of general managerial knowledge and capabilities between the merging firms

Some other benefits from the combination usually do not require special managerial skills, such as increased bargaining power vis-a-vis suppliers just from combining purchases of both companies. The next sections describe the various sources of synergy.

Sharing Resources

Combining units, departments, and functions, and eliminating redundant activities can bring significant cost reductions. For example, using one sales force to sell similar products and services rather than two forces can generate significant cost-savings. Similarly, unifying national and international distribution channels can help streamline processes and save millions of dollars annually. Using the same manufacturing facilities, human resource departments, finance and accounting services, purchasing activities, inbound and outbound logistics facilities, and information technology networks can also contribute to a significant reduction in operating expenses and improvement in operational efficiency.

The joint use of shared services by the merged company can enhance and sustain its competitive advantage by reducing costs that result from economies of scale, efficient allocation and use of resources, and accelerated running on the learning curve.

One of the main reasons commonly cited as to why resistance to cooperation occurs following a merger is the removal of managerial autonomy in the acquired firms. The need to coordinate with, report to, and be controlled by the acquiring body can reduce the sense of freedom and autonomy of the acquired company's managers to the point of insubordination and thus diminish or even nullify the expected benefits of the M&A.

This and related issues of behavior, level of integration, and ways to deal with these effects are discussed in the chapters in Part IV, "Post-Merger Integration and Implementation." Thus, considerations of the degree of post–merger integration (PMI) between combining firms and the resultant degree of autonomy removal that can affect the exploitation of the anticipated synergy potential are important issues that need to be considered in planning and implementing of activities to seize potential synergies.

Knowledge, Skills, and Capabilities Transfer

Knowledge and best practices transferred from one company to another can bring an increase in revenues and a decrease in costs. There are many options for knowledge and best practices transfer. Intellectual property of the firms concerning R&D management, product design, and the manufacturing process is an invaluable source of a sustainable competitive advantage. Knowledge pertaining to skilled staff availability, effective use of distribution channels, supplier base, and sources of financing also contribute to the strength of the merged entities. The basic idea is that one or both entities improve their competitive advantage through a learning process that entails the transfer of complementary functional competencies between the merging firms.

The transfer of knowledge and functional skills and capabilities is a rather complex process. Many times, the highly specialized tacit knowledge and skills that are the domain of individuals and teams in the acquired organization are not well documented (not codified), and thus difficult to imitate. Hence, willingness and an ability to both teach and learn from the other party are of paramount importance in added value creation through M&As.

Yet, if knowledge transfer is successful, it is a great source of synergy and the main reason for the M&A. Therefore, special attention is given here for these processes.

Basically, *knowledge transfer* refers to the transfer of experience or ways to accomplish things. It includes the process of organizing, creating, capturing, and distributing knowledge between parties, along with making it available for future use. Essentially, this is a matter of accomplishing future work together, or of allowing someone else to take on a task and potentially develop it further. In an acquisition of a company, it might well be the case that what is actually acquired are the skills of key staff or advanced technology that needs to be integrated with present solutions.

Types of Knowledge

Knowledge comes about in many different forms and for many different reasons. It could be thought of as explicit or tacit, meaning that it is either "tangible" and easy to document, or much more in the heads of its carriers. Knowledge could further be divided into embrained, embodied, encultured, embedded, and encoded, along a similar axis of explicitness and tacitness. *Embrained knowledge* describes knowledge that is dependent on cognitive and conceptual skills. *Embodied knowledge* consists of contextual practices and is socially and action-oriented. *Encultured knowledge* refers to how parties achieve and share understandings through socialization and acculturation. *Embedded knowledge* is contained within systematic routines and relates to such routines, roles, and so on. *Encoded knowledge* is explicit and in the form of signs, symbols, and different types of devices.

Knowledge can further be understood on the organizational or individual level, or as a combination of the two. Knowledge embedded in devices could be considered as organizational, while it could also be argued that it is always individuals that interpret and use the knowledge. Again, the knowledge embedded in devices might not exist beyond the organization and could hence not be carried forth by individuals. The knowledge that is individual draws attention to how changes in the staff—planned reorganizations as well as staff that decide to leave following the M&A—impact the knowledge transfer. Although it might be rational to decrease the number of staff, and although it might be wise to actually let some managers go to accomplish change, it can have severe effects on the knowledge kept and maintained by the organization. Such decisions need to be reflected in light of the importance of the knowledge to the M&A. As a rule of thumb, the more the acquired party is knowledge-intensive (hi-tech), and the more the business is focused on services as opposed to production, the more important it would be to maintain the staff. In the latter circumstance, this also links to the retention of customers.

Knowledge Transfer Process

The *knowledge transfer process* entails the assessment of the knowledge, its sharing, and assimilation. These steps can be further divided into the identification of the knowledge holders within the organization, the motivation of the knowledge holders to share, the creation of a mechanism to accomplish the knowledge transfer, the actual knowledge transfer execution, measurements to ensure the transfer, and the application of the transferred knowledge at its new locations.

Tools to help accomplish the transfer of knowledge include simulation, joint work or work shadowing, practices, narratives, mentorship, communities, guided experience, guided experimentation, and paired work. Some of these fit better to a specific kind of knowledge than others. For instance, the transfer of explicit knowledge can be accomplished through simple information and documentation, whereas the more fluid knowledge requires repeated interactions and mentorships. It can, however, be easier to facilitate through documentation and codification.

The knowledge transfer following an M&A needs to be consciously planned and integrated with other activities, such as the social integration of individuals, cultural concerns, leadership, and communication. These issues are discussed at length in Part IV.

Items of knowledge should be mapped, and if possible documented, or else acknowledged in terms of who carries the knowledge and how measures (in terms of benefits and so on) can be taken to ascertain that key people commit to the M&A and the new organization. To decrease vulnerability, knowledge carried by individual staff members should be analyzed and considered in terms of how it can be shared or documented. This process of knowledge transfer depends on the positive attitudes of people toward this process, and entails the creation of trust in the leaders, the M&A vision, and in the other party. It can take some time which needs to be allowed. Communication is one important part of the creation of trust, as is the social interaction among individuals that are to share the knowledge. In the creation of mechanisms to enable the knowledge transfer, different schemes need to run in parallel. These include socialization processes between individuals, communication, and so on to establish trust, and the organizing of meetings, communities, and so forth to facilitate the knowledge exchange. It also entails the creation of structures and possible documentation to support the knowledge transfer.

Issues of Knowledge Transfer

Certain kinds of knowledge are more easily handled and transferred: explicit (codified) knowledge allows itself to be documented and can also more easily be separated from its carriers. Such knowledge can be documented and transferred through manuals, working methods, instructions, and similar ways. Tacit knowledge is a more complex type of knowledge to transfer. It might be that the carrier of the knowledge is not even aware of its existence, and it cannot easily be documented. It resides in organizational members, artifacts, tools, tasks, and so on, which also means that it might be more or less easy to transfer in terms of who has the knowledge and who is to receive it, the type of knowledge, and how well it fits with current knowledge of the recipient. Organizational devices can help to a certain extent, either for the actual transfer of the knowledge, or at least to increase awareness of its existence.

Other issues that complicate knowledge transfer are distances between parties: geographical, cultural, organizational, and knowledge-based distances that make it more complex to understand the other party and interpret the knowledge. Such distances can become apparent following a merger or acquisition and are especially salient if it is an international acquisition. The lack of shared values or identities complicates the general knowledge transfer and similarly so, such absence of shared values might well be the consequence of a merger or acquisition. This also links the knowledge transfer to the integration of cultures and identities, and points to how to a certain extent such integrations need to precede the knowledge transfer, while the knowledge transfer is also part of the integration of cultures (transfer of such items as values). Language barriers can negatively impact the knowledge transfer, which once again relates to issues that follow from international acquisitions.

One complicating factor in knowledge transfer is how well the knowledge matches the current knowledge of the party that is to receive the knowledge. If the receiver has too little knowledge related to what is transferred, he might find it difficult to make any meaning of the new knowledge items. This calls for certain levels of overlaps in terms of knowledge and skills among parties to make the knowledge transferable. If the knowledge is similar, the new knowledge does not contribute much to the recipient. If it is too diverse, the receiving party cannot understand and make the best use of the knowledge. Complementarity would hence be important, where similar knowledge structures and values can help the receiving party to understand a somewhat more diverse knowledge.

Enable Knowledge Transfer

There are several aspects that ease or enable the transfer of knowledge. Some of these aspects are determined in the choice of the target, other ones through how the actual knowledge transfer is pursued, and some stem from the acquirer's ability to handle acquisitions. Starting with the last aspect, it seems that acquirers that have previous experience from M&As are better at handling later ones. This suggests that knowledge on how to acquire is collected by the organization and used in later instances. It also points to how wiser choices in terms of targets can be made based on previous mistakes. The knowledge on how to acquire should ideally be documented to make it more explicit, and also so it can be used by different parties in the organization. The defence-delivering firm Alpha has created a specific unit within the firm to handle its acquisitions. That unit engages directly with potential targets on a demand-driven basis to support different divisions of the defence-delivering firm. In addition, it also works to think ahead and find more radical solutions that might fit with the product portfolio and competencies of the firm.

In addition to the knowledge on M&As, it is important how the knowledge of the acquired party relates to that of the acquirer. The knowledge bases need to be compatible to needs, interpretations of existing experiences, and values, and they should also be complementary. An acquirer that develops skills in how to take on knowledge from other parties will be better off for the transfer of knowledge from future targets. This can partly happen through learning from previous mergers or acquisitions but can also be developed in a more general sense as absorptive capabilities.

Looking at the aspect of how the knowledge transfer is handled, socialization among parties helps. It is also important that the staff remains with the company. This specifically applies to managers and key personnel, which then links knowledge transfer to motivation, communication, and the establishment of trust. The more explicit knowledge can be transferred by documentation, whereas the tacit needs socialization and communities. These can also support the transfer of the explicit knowledge in how they break down differences or bring attention to them. Another important aspect of how the knowledge transfer is handled, which relates to the parties involved, is that of unlearning. To take on new knowledge, an organization needs to unlearn previous methods or ways. This does not relate to when the knowledge is tacit and relates to values and cultures. Habits, cognitive structures, and values need to be replaced. Such processes must be allowed to take time, while they should be prioritized. Ways to unlearn include visions and motivations to reach to a "better state," and organizational artifacts that disable the continuation of previous structures and ways of acting.

Knowledge transfer in international acquisitions is enabled by committing key people, allowing for staff and managers to rotate jobs, interacting and exchanging ideas among them, addressing cultural differences, and facilitating information exchange. These parameters would help in the establishment of trust among parties and would also raise the awareness of how communication might be understood differently among parties. In addition, it is important to bring forth how the culture is different between the companies and their nations. Although integration might be resisted, the pure awareness of such differences eases communication and might create trust rather than distrust.

Knowledge Transfer in Technology and Innovation-Intensive Acquisitions

In the acquisition of knowledge-intensive firms, such as innovative companies, start-ups, biomedical engineering firms, and so on, the transfer of knowledge is an essential component. Often such firms are acquired to strengthen the innovation pipeline and/ or utilize the skills of the staff. In the latter circumstance, it is frequently argued that the acquired party should be kept autonomous following the acquisition. This is the case so as not to destroy values of the firm, make staff stay on, and also potentially not change interaction partners with co-innovators. It is also the circumstance of how the acquirer might lack the absorptive capacities needed to assimilate the knowledge.

Evidence exists that integration will make staff less productive or innovative. This follows from how the innovative staff needs the freedom to be creative; while such freedom is impeded by the integration, it can also be integrated only to a limited extent. These results are not entirely inconclusive however, and the more targeted routines of an acquirer can actually help to bring innovations to market and make the innovative firms more focused.

Some studies have shown that when the innovative firm is not integrated with its acquirer, its innovative capability can be lost. Here, such issues as choosing a target that is not in too early a development phase, ensuring that the founders (innovators) continue with the company for some time, while potentially disbanding later to allow for the future growth of the firm, and also ensuring that network parties continue with the firm to as high an extent as possible. In line with increased focus on co-creation, all innovative skills might not be entirely part of the innovative firm and hence, its reliance on external parties and networking continue to be important following an acquisition. Network parties might however feel that their roles have been replaced by the acquirer in terms of providing support to the innovative firm, or they might find conflicts in interacting— directly or indirectly—with the acquirer (Öberg et al., 2011). As a consequence, they disband. It is thereby important to take measures to avoid such disbanding because it can have severe consequences for the innovative firm and its future ability to bring forth new ideas, as does the risk of staff leaving the firm. A recent study (Öberg, 2013) points to how acquirers can benefit from imitating the innovative firms' network parties in the acquisition and integration of firms. This relates to how an innovative firm often has pre-acquisition collaborations with mature firms that do not seem to decrease the freedom or creativity of the innovative firm. Such mature firms, in turn, have created capacities to interact through developing subunits that share or complement visions of the innovative firms, while creating a gap within these firms between their well-established way of pursuing business and their interaction with innovative firms. An acquirer can to a similar extent create such subunits and hence bring differences in interaction patterns into the firm rather than have it on the interface with the innovative, acquired parties.

Knowledge Transfer of General Management Skills and Capabilities

In addition to knowledge transfer between functions and units of the two companies, an M&A can assist in enhancing the ability of top management of one company to make quality decisions on formulating long-term goals and various strategic alternatives, systematic strategic choice processes that help to decide on the appropriate strategic direction, define a strategic vision and business mission, and devise and implement the strategic course of action. Other benefits might be related to organizational planning and coordinating, designing control and evaluation systems, using an appropriate organizational structure, and using analytical tools for financial and strategic planning. As an example, the merger between Hoechst and Rhone–Poulence that created Aventis involved the transfer of managerial skills and abilities between merging companies, and also allowed the new entity to exploit the economies of scale and scope.

Other Benefits of the M&A

Although the previously mentioned areas of synergy require substantial efforts for identifying and realizing them, there are some relatively easy gains that can be obtained by the very nature of the merger.

First, better purchasing power through economies of scale is often achieved, leading to lowering purchasing costs. Second, the brand name, product positioning, and distribution channels of the unified company can be utilized to command higher prices and to increase sales volume. Third, a bigger corporate entity might have better recruiting attractiveness and greater access to financial resources. Fourth, there could be taxation advantages and better use of cash reserves. Needless to say, that in a case of horizontal integration (M&A between rival firms), the intensity of competition is potentially lowered, and the market share of an amalgamated entity can be increased. The potential benefits in this particular area are often overstated. This is because the extent and nature of the competitive response from the remaining competitors in the market is underestimated. It is also possible that regulatory requirements imposed by competition authorities (for example, the requirement to dispose of certain entities or product lines) will place limits on the possible benefits achievable.

Last, but not least, it is common to use new M&As as a platform to gain access to new technological areas that seem to be promising. Examples include Google's purchase of Admob (2009) and Apple's acquisition of Quattro (2010). An initial acquisition can bring about other acquisitions, which are often combined with internal development that eventually generates a major presence in the new technological area. In recent years, this has been particularly prevalent as companies seek to gain access to rapidly developing technologies as opposed to building both the technology and then market share.

Analysis of Synergy Potential

The identification of the potential for synergy should initially be assessed before deal closure. This will influence the price to be paid, the nature and difficulty associated with the integration program, and the level of change in the organizations post-acquisition. At times, because of the necessity for quick action and confidentiality required, the detailed analysis of synergy potential is made immediately after the M&A agreement is sealed. Whatever the circumstances are, the operations of both merging entities should be identified and compared.

In previous chapters, the differences between different types of mergers, such as vertical integration and horizontal integration, were briefly discussed. It is useful to elaborate further here on certain aspects of the different types of mergers to assist in understanding opportunities for synergies. This elaboration also includes advantages and disadvantages of the different types of mergers as related to realization of synergy potential.

Horizontal Mergers

The analysis of synergy potential starts with horizontal mergers with the highest potential for synergy. The acquisition of competitors or complementary products reflect horizontal integration and is a related merger. Related mergers occur when the acquiring company and the acquired company where the industry in which they operate is related. Figure 5.1 illustrates the analysis of synergy potential as a result of combining business units and departments to cut costs in a merger of two companies in the same industry. Also it shows examples of the transfer of capabilities and knowledge between departments (see arrows).

This comparative assessment of mutual strengths and weaknesses should be aided by using the value-chain analysis (see Chapter 3, "Strategic Motives and Considerations," for explanations on the value-chain method) which describes the main activities such as R&D, manufacturing, marketing, distribution, after-sale service and support, as well as the supporting activities, such as accounting and finance, human resources, information systems, and others. Each of these activities can become a probable synergy area because of the operational cooperation or due to the transfer of knowledge and skills.

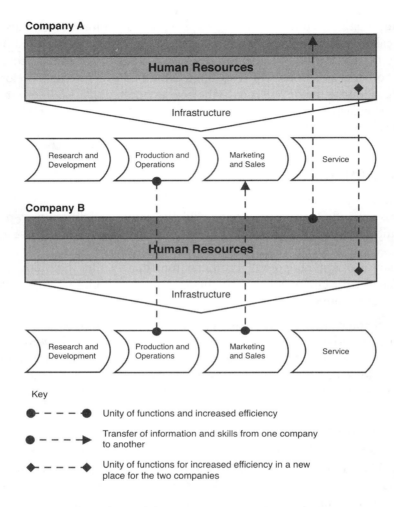

Figure 5.1   Analysis of the Synergy Potential Among Competitors
(Adapted from Weber, 2003)

Vertical Integration

The acquisition of the supplier and the acquisition of the client are examples of vertical integration. This section primarily discusses the advantages and disadvantages of vertical integrations.

In many cases, managers believe that it is cheaper, less dangerous, and easier to perform the work of coordinating between the functions in the organization when these functions are included in the company's organizational framework and are controlled by the management. This situation is in contrast to the alternatives of making agreements and the performance of transactions in the market, the creation of strategic alliances, or the establishment of a joint venture. For instance, where the sales and distribution functions are performed by the organization using its own sales people as opposed to using another independent organization that specializes in marketing and distribution. If the company has not operated until now in distribution and sales, it can begin to do so (internal development) or it can acquire a distribution and sales company. Thus, the merger is called a forward vertical integration, which is drawing closer to the final customer. This is what the Elco Company did when it acquired Sensor and then Shekem and expanded Shekem Electric.

Other possibilities of forward vertical integration are the acquisition of a transport company (to move the company's products), the acquisition of a company for marketing information and market analysis, and the acquisition of a company for providing services and performing repairs for the company's products.

The acquisition of companies that provide the raw materials is called backward vertical integration. Additional possibilities of backward vertical integration include the acquisition of the company that provides the machinery for manufacturing, the acquisition of the producer of the machinery, the acquisition of the producer and/or the supplier of the parts, the acquisition of a company for research and development of products and processes, the acquisition of a financing company, and the acquisition of a company that transports the raw materials. In certain industries, there are companies with complete vertical integration. For example, in the paper industry, there are companies that engage in the full range of activities—they raise the trees in the forests, they cut down the trees, they prepare the pulp from the trees, they process the pulp for different levels of paper, and they distribute the paper to business and private customers.

Saving on Expenses

Many expenses are saved when the organization plans, coordinates, and supervises, by itself, the acquisition, the production, the sales, the marketing, and so on. The costs of transport can be saved through the appropriate placement of the facilities, like in the case of companies that use sulphuric acid (fertilizers and fuel), where the costs of transporting hazardous materials are significant.

Vertical integration saves on the costs of the coordination and supervision that the organization needs to perform with suppliers or distributors. In addition, the organization has costs of data collection and analysis regarding the market, the sales and demand forecasts, information on raw materials and different suppliers, and so on. All these provide areas for saving following a vertical integration. Additional costs that can be saved are associated with publicity, sales and marketing personnel, purchasing department, negotiation and price comparison costs, product quality management, packing, specifications, and more.

Assurance of Supply or Demand

Vertical integration can assure that the company has sales when the demand is low and/ or that the company has a supply of raw materials and essential products of requisite quality even in periods of limited supply. For instance, the Coca-Cola Company depends on CO_2 for the quality of its beverage. Although the costs of the gas are low in comparison to other costs, the lack of the gas can prevent the production and sale of the beverage. Therefore, collaboration or ownership of the production is, in this case, critical.

In the same industry, PepsiCo acquired fast food chains—Pizza Hut, Kentucky Fried Chicken, and Taco Bell—and thus assured a considerable percentage of its sales in the important fast food market. The assurance of supply and sales reduces uncertainty and risks and enables a more comfortable bargaining position with other suppliers or customers. Another example is Tnuva's acquisition of Anvei Zion at the end of 2002 to ensure the supply of high-quality fruit for Tnuva's successful product, Yoplait yogurts. Tnuva could have imported the fruit, but issues associated with transport, storage, fruit freshness, and fruit quality are more easily managed by having control over the supply of this essential component.

Thus, vertical integration enables protection against the actions of competitors that might take control over sources of supply or channels of distribution. Even if they acquire only the quality suppliers or distributors, they leave the rest of the competitors at an inferior position. Even a decline in the number of suppliers or distributors reduces the bargaining power of the other competitors.

Improvement of Competitive Advantage

Understanding the different elements associated with the costs of production of raw materials, other key components, along with plant and machinery and the savings that can be achieved, can enable the company to set more competitive prices and create cost advantages. Conversely, the organization can improve the differentiation of its products and achieve additional market segments and sell at higher prices than those of the competitors. The company can better manage the distribution and solve logistical problems for its clients and provide better service/products, unique and targeted to its customers.

In addition, vertical integration creates higher entry barriers. A new company that enters the industry suffers from a position of inferiority given these aforementioned advantages of a company with forward and backward vertical integration. If a new company were to want to perform vertical integrations, the entry barrier is even higher.

For potential synergy in vertical integration, see Figure 5.2.

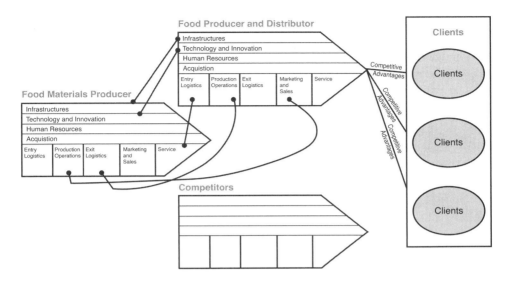

Figure 5.2   Synergy Potential in Vertical Integration Between Supplier
and Producer (Weber, Y. 2003)

Disadvantages of Vertical Integration

Increased Costs

In addition to an increase in bureaucratic costs relating to coordination between the acquiring and acquired company's management, there might be other costs, for example, where there is a requirement to purchase from a company-owned supplier. This might mean that the company does not check for cheaper suppliers or bargain on prices or terms. Moreover, the supplier in the corporation, which is accustomed to selling to customers in the corporation framework, might not work as hard to improve product or supply quality as its competitors and thus might become less effective and efficient, and have high costs and prices. For example, at the start of the 1990s, General Motors acquired 68 percent of the car components from within the corporation, more than any other company. (Chrysler acquired 30 percent and Toyota 28 percent.) General Motors was the manufacturer with the highest costs in the industry. In 1992, General Motors paid $34.6 an hour to workers who worked in the supplier companies it owned while its competitors paid one-half this figure.

Decline in Flexibility of Change of Suppliers or Customers

In the event of technological changes, changes in components, decline in product quality, and decline in the supplier management ability, companies tend to change suppliers. However, if the supplier is another organization within the corporation, there is often no rush to change it, and eventually the acquiring company's competitive ability is negatively impacted. The problem is especially prominent in the situation of rapid technological changes in which the company might find itself stuck with a supplier with outdated technology and products.

In addition, if there are fluctuations of supply or demand to one of the companies in the corporation chain, the balance in the production and supply for other companies in the corporation can be disrupted. It is not simple to maintain balanced output in a corporation.

Erroneous Perceptions

There are a number of erroneous perceptions and assumptions regarding vertical integration. The assumption that it is possible to transfer a good reputation to another business is not always realized. The assumption that it is always more economical to perform activities within the one corporate group is also not fulfilled in many cases. Outsourcing shows that in many cases it is preferable to perform the activities through a specialized external party. Some management teams believe that experience and knowledge in one part of the chain can help it manage the business of its supplier or the customer in another part of the chain. In the case of PepsiCo, its management did not have a real contribution to the fast food chains it acquired.

Interim conclusion: Although the previously discussed analysis is done at times, the main scientific insights to date indicate that corporate entities that go through an M&A fail to fully integrate their respective operations, and, thus, fail to use the synergies previously indicated. For a summary of the synergy potential on all areas of synergy and on both cost effectiveness and growth potential, see Table 5.1.

Table 5.1   Examples of Synergy Potential (Adapted from Weber, 2003)

	Increase of Effectiveness and Reduction of Costs	Increase in Sales and Market Shares
Sharing Operations Resources	■ Savings in logistical costs, shared cooling warehouses, and containers were used. ■ Savings in inspection and coordination. ■ Savings in data collection. ■ Due to stable relations—development of unique efficient procedures.	**Quality improves reputation and sales** ■ Increase of sales in existing segments/existing products ■ Increase of market share ■ Other products and delicacies ■ Addition of market segments **Distribution and Marketing** ■ Entry into additional areas, such as cooled foods, children's food, desserts, and baked goods.
Transfer of Professional Skills in Functions	**Research and Development** ■ Access to technology ■ More rapid development pace ■ Shorter time to market ■ Efficient R&D management ■ Operations-computerization of production processes	**Research and Development** ■ Acquisition of skills of R&D in the processed food area. ■ Acquisition of knowledge in the area of food without preservatives. **Marketing** ■ Analysis and fit to the clients' tastes. (See the regular successes in the taste tests.)
Transfer of Economic Management Skills and Competitive Advantages	■ Increased height of entry barriers ■ Protection against blocks ■ Reduction of risk and uncertainty in supply	■ Reduction of risk and uncertainty in supply. ■ Improved differentiation ability. ■ Increase of entry barriers. ■ Saving and increased efficiency improves competitive ability with clients.

Although M&As can yield a number of benefits, they can have a range of other consequences which will be discussed in the next chapter.

References

Öberg, C. (2011). Acquiring once, acquiring twice - Lessons learned from repeated acquisitions of innovative firms. *International Journal of Innovation Management*, 15 (6), 1243-1269.

Öberg, C., Grundström, C., & Jönsson, P. (2011). Acquisitions and network identity change. *European Journal of Marketing*, 45 (9/10), 1470-1500.

Öberg, C. (2013). Network imitation to deal with socio-cultural dilemmas in acquisitions of young, innovative firms. *Thunderbird International Business Review*, 55 (4), 387-403.

Weber, Y. (2003). *Mergers and acquisitions management*. Peles:Rishon LeTzion (In Hebrew).

6

CULTURE AND CULTURAL DIFFERENCES ANALYSIS

"There is a good way and a bad way to address the implementation of mergers and acquisitions. Both require the same efforts and the same investment time. The difference is that one way succeeds and the other way fails."
—CEO of a consumer goods company

Introduction

The surprising factor in an era when it is known that M&As have a high failure rate is not that the organizational culture is a key factor for success. The surprise is that organizational culture differences have yet to become a main factor in the process of decision making of directors and senior management in the choice of appropriate M&As, in the determination of the value of the transaction, in the planning of the integration of the two organizations, and in the retention of the human capital of the acquired company that tends to leave immediately after the merger. No wonder why a report of Boston Consulting Group (BCG) from 2010 states that acquirers should conduct a cultural diagnosis of the two companies to systematically analyze and understand the true nature of the differences between the two parties' cultures, and the differences should be systematically mapped out and prioritized. But how can you do this analysis? What are the method and measurement tools? When and how should you use the results of systematic analysis? This chapter answers all these questions.

Chapter 5, "Synergy Potential and Realization," discusses the primary management-based reason for the performance of the M&A, namely, the realization of the potential of synergy. This chapter discusses challenges and difficulties that might be encountered during the process of synergy realization. Thus, this chapter focuses on cultural differences analysis for the purpose of screening, classifying, and examining the fit of the potential acquired companies to the acquiring company. Actually, the use of cultural differences analysis should be considered in all stages of the M&A.

The Importance and Advantages of Evaluation and Measurement of Differences of Management Culture

Many managers already know that it is far easier to close an M&A deal than to implement it in the years following the signing of the agreement. Countless research studies and surveys of senior managers show again and again that the main factor that can cause the integration of the organizations to fail is differences in management culture and their implications on the human factor, such as the departure of managers and key personnel from the acquired company.

For example, 20 out of 25 of the senior managers of Scitex left the company in the first year after its acquisition by Creo, despite the efforts and persuasion attempts to retain them in the merged company. In this case, there are also differences of national culture that, apparently, contributed to the implementation difficulties.

According to the former VP of HR of Teva Pharmaceutical Industries (the world's largest generic pharmaceutical company) Mr. Haim Benjamini:

> It is necessary to deal with the cultural aspect of every merger and acquisition as if it were due diligence. You have to go out into the field, wander among the people, and learn every pertinent detail, such as: What is the management culture? Is it centralized or decentralized? (Maltz, 2003)

Benjamini also notes that there are organizational cultural differences of organizations in different states within the United States. Although it is only 5 hours flying time between Pennsylvania and California, there are cultural differences between the two states. "Just because both are part of the [United States], that doesn't mean that they have the same culture, as we've learned over time" (Maltz, 2003).

Cross-cultural management is an essential key success factor in the post-merger integration (PMI) of two organizations. It is surprising, therefore, that organizational culture differences have yet to become part of the decision-making process of directors and senior management regarding such matters as screening and finding the appropriate M&A, determining the value and price of the transaction, planning the integration process of the two organizations, as well as retaining the human capital of the target company, who tends to leave shortly after the deal is signed.

One of the main reasons that corporate cultural differences are not properly evaluated in the pre-merger period, not considered during the negotiation stage, and not used in the integration process is the use of a broad spectrum of consultants. The overwhelming and multifaceted complexity of the M&A process analysis necessitates many experts from various disciplines such as accounting, finance, auditing, legal, investment banking, psychologists, and so on. For instance, in the planning stage, before the deal is signed, transaction advisors typically drive the process without the involvement of HR experts and PMI consultants.

Ideally, the consultant's interventions should span all stages of the M&A process. In many unsuccessful mergers, the assessment of integration process challenges and related HR problems due to culture clash remains outside the decision-making process at the pre-merger and negotiation stage. Whereas in a successful M&A, the assessment done at the pre-merger stage is implemented immediately after the deal is closed.

Many mergers also fail because of a lack of methodical and thorough measurement of the culture differences. One of the more well-known examples is the acquisition of NCR by AT&T in the beginning of the 1990s. The centralized management of NCR did not suit the openness and creativity of AT&T. Eventually, NCR was sold at one-half its market value and AT&T lost 3 billion dollars. In contrast, there are opposite cases, such as the acquisition of the Morris Aviation Company by the Southwest Aviation Company. Here the acquiring company invested 2 months in learning the culture before the agreement and ended the integration process within 11 months, instead of the 3 years determined by initial evaluations.

What Is Organizational Culture?

The word *culture* has many meanings, various connotations, and different definitions without unequivocal agreement among different researchers. However, one definition of management culture indicates the ability to predict many phenomena, including success or failure of M&As. According to this definition, management culture is a *developing system of beliefs (as well as values and assumptions) that is shared by the managers regarding the desired way of management for the organization so that it can deal with the adjustment to its environment.*

As detailed in this chapter, this definition focuses on the process of measurement and analysis of the management of the organization. The focus on the management's approaches and management style has many advantages in M&As. In addition, it is possible to measure and evaluate the culture at relatively low costs. The definition focuses on beliefs, values, and fundamental assumptions; although, other definitions also include ceremonies, garb, and other apparent aspects of the organization. However, what is important to M&As is included in the definition and the rest provides further information for the confirmation of the findings.

The system of beliefs and fundamental assumptions—of work methods and approaches that lead to success—develop from the accumulated experience of the organization management and its workers during dealing with the competition and different factors in the environment. This type of dealing with management challenges entails interpreting information collected and adopting actions on the basis of such interpretations. Thus, culture is an acquired system of knowledge and frameworks of reference that enable the understanding and explanation of what occurs in the organization, in the sector, and in the world. Therefore, management culture is critical in preparing programs and making decisions to cope with ongoing different management challenges. Because the interpretations depend on additional factors, such as the nature and background of the people, the actions undertaken, and the interpretations of the success of these actions, every group of people, and namely every manager, will develop a different management culture even when the organizations and their management operate in the same sector and in the same country.

All the beliefs, assumptions, and fundamental hypotheses of the management become a complete system with unique content that shapes the processes of decision making and influences the choice of strategies, policy, principles, and all behaviors in the organization. Thus, for example, research on the manner of decision making of the senior management reported that one management group decided upon its financial goals while significantly increasing its debts. This course of action derived from the different beliefs and assumptions of the two managements regarding the risk that should be taken during strategic operations. Assumptions of this type influence, for instance, the levels of investment in areas of research and development in different projects, the inspection processes, the level of autonomy given to managers, the organizational structure, and many actions adopted by different divisions in the organization.

The system of beliefs, which constitutes the organizational culture, operates as a filter through which the people in the organization perceive the reality with which the organization deals, and thus it fills two essential roles. First, the system of beliefs enables the complex world and the considerable uncertainty to be translated into familiar, comprehensible terms. Second, the system of beliefs provides continuity and stability when changes threaten to undermine the knowledge accumulated from experience. Thus, the culture constitutes control functions for deviations from the knowledge and experience that have been acquired. However, as previously noted and as will be seen in this chapter, these roles make the culture important to those who hold it, make it difficult to implement required change, and become an essential basis for the conflict between the two cultures that meet in an M&A.

Dimensions of Organizational Culture

Top management teams hold numerous beliefs and basic assumptions. Nevertheless, the literature and the research studies indicate that you can isolate a number of important assumptions and beliefs that characterize cultures of organizations. Beliefs are not necessarily good, correct, or bad, and the proof is that in the same industry you can find a number of successful organizations in which each has its own different culture.

Most important, these beliefs and assumptions have the power to predict critical phenomena that influence the success of the M&A. The experience in measuring differences in management culture shows that the different beliefs and assumptions can be collected into seven areas that constitute the dimensions of organizational/management culture.

1. Approach to Innovation and Activity

Managers with a strong orientation for innovation and dynamic activity encourage a rapid response to changes and to competition in the outside environment. In addition, they encourage innovation to cope with what exists in an environment and win the competition. They attempt to exploit opportunities for new products and markets. In contrast, in organizations that are different in terms of their management culture, the managers prefer stability, intensive planning, and a relatively high level of formality. They do not want to run and grasp at every opportunity because of the risk entailed by the uncertainty, and they hold to the adage by author St. Jerome that "Haste is of the Devil." In addition, the difference in management approaches derives from the fact that there are different perceptions regarding the urgency required for activity and response to changes.

2. Approach to Risk-Taking

The management philosophy and the beliefs regarding taking risks are main factors that differentiate between organizations. The tendency to take risks influences many decisions, such as investments in new initiatives, acquisition and investments in production equipment and technologies, the level of investment in research and development, management of cash flow and credit, and even the way in which the worker pension funds are run.

For this dimension and its predecessor, the approach to activity and innovation, a relatively high correlation was found. For instance, the achievement of a competitive advantage using innovation requires investment in R&D, which can be risky because of the lack of success and lack of uncertainty in the development ability, required time, and fit to market. In essence, the degree of perceived urgency indicates the perception of the threat and the risk in the lack of activity or response. This is also true for the exploitation of opportunities. In other words, the degree of urgency derived from the approach to risk influences the approach to the need for activity and dynamism.

3. Lateral Interdependence: Horizontal Relationship

Managements have different managerial approaches in beliefs about the importance of cooperation and attachment between the organizational units for the achievement of the organization's goals or the encouragement of competition between them to increase

--■

motivation and effort. Some organizations have complex coordination mechanisms, whereas others use simple means of coordination, such as schedules and standardization. The importance ascribed by the managements to cooperation and communication is reflected in encouraging knowledge sharing, understanding the difficulties and problems that the parallel position-holder has, and help offered to other organizational units as opposed to the competition. Obviously, there are also managements that encourage competition, in the spirit of "envy inspires wisdom."

4. Top Management Contact: Vertical-Hierarchical Contact

This dimension addresses the management's beliefs regarding the attitude toward the subordinates, for example, support, warmth, understanding, and encouragement. These beliefs address human nature in organizations and thus are different from one management to another, as according to the X and Y theories that were prevalent in the past. The assumption that people let go, become lazy, and avoid responsibility, as in the X theory, leads to an organizational culture different from that in another organization that treats its people in an opposite manner, as in the Y theory.

Thus, managements will differ in their beliefs regarding the encouragement that should be given to subordinates to attempt new ideas, to be creative, and to take risks. In the same way, there will be different management approaches that enable workers to overtly criticize the management or bring up conflicts to be discussed.

5. Autonomy and Decision Making

A basic characteristic of managements is the different belief of the level of autonomy and responsibility that should be delegated in important decisions. These beliefs influence, in the end, the form of the organizational structure. They influence the definitions of the roles, the definitions of the procedures, and the level of formality in these definitions.

6. Approach to Performances

Characterizing the requirements of managers and workers and focusing on evaluating performances are especially important aspects for different managements. Here the managements differ in their beliefs regarding the need to require constant improvement and to achieve goals, even challenging ones. Thus, in one of the well-known hi-tech companies in Israel, the motto is "can do—will do." In other words, everything that can be done will be done, despite the difficulty. Other beliefs address the importance of the requirement from managers to bear responsibility for their performances and the requirement that expectations of performances will be clear and measurable. Other emphases address the types of performances, such as the requirement for efficiency and the manner of task performance as opposed to the requirement for effectiveness and the achievement of all goals, even at the expense of efficiency.

7. Approach to Rewards

The management culture is expressed in the manner of reward. The answer to the question of "Who is rewarded and why?" is a clear declaration regarding the beliefs and values preferred by the management. The approach of rewards is related to beliefs of the need to reward fairly and competitively in relation to other organizations in the industry. In addition, part of this dimension is the belief in the need to link between reward and performance and the extent to which this relationship is emphasized in salary, benefits, and other related aspects.

As aforementioned, these dimensions of culture can greatly predict the behavior phenomena of managers, including their departure from the organization, as well as the expected success of the merger. However, other areas are also important to the understanding to the management/organizational culture. This understanding is required for analyzing the situation before the agreement and for the need to prepare change programs and deal with the differences in culture after the agreement in the process of integrating the organizations. These additional areas are consideration of the systems of work relations and the weight of the worker committees in the organization. In addition, the ownership of the organization, family versus public, greatly influences the nature and management of the organization. Table 6.1 shows cultural differences in other areas of activity as presented to the CEO of company M that considered a merger with company H, in addition to the seven regular dimensions of organizational culture that already have been described.

It is necessary to emphasize that there is no "good" or "bad" in terms of the preferences of the management and its beliefs. However, there can be a certain management culture that is not suited for activity in an industry, and thus the organization's performances will be poor. In other words, the management/organizational culture is related to the organization's performances, but there is no "one-and-only" culture that brings about a high level of performance; rather, there can be a number of management cultures that each lead the organization to good performances.

The seven dimensions of culture are also significant when mergers between organizations from different countries are examined. For international mergers, you must also examine, *in addition to* the seven dimensions, international differences of culture.

For example, in a merger deal between German FAST and Israeli Aladdin in 1995, there were many differences. According to the former CEO of Aladdin Mr. Yanki Margalit:

> In the first meetings, it was hard to sweep the stereotypes under the rug. Like the stereotype that Israelis believe in—that Germans are square and orderly, while they themselves are the kings of improvisation (Gomes et al., 2011).

Beyond the national cultural differences between Germany and Israel, in the case of Aladdin and FAST, there were also significant frictions based on corporate culture differences. The prominent example was in the marketing division, where there were considerable conceptual differences regarding the degree of involvement and aggressiveness. In the German-speaking market, FAST was marketing successfully and professionally. However, the marketing vice-CEO of Aladdin nevertheless was attempting to educate FAST's marketing managers to evince greater aggressiveness (Gomes et al., 2011).

Some national differences were measured and are known such as the five dimensions suggested by Hofstede (Hofstede 1980). However, as already has been stated regarding local mergers, it is necessary to examine additional aspects and other areas of activity that can constitute difficulties in the integration processes of organizations (see Table 6.1).

Table 6.1   Differences in Corporate Culture (in Addition to the Seven Dimensions of Culture)

Areas of Activity	Company M		Company H
Structure and decisions	Decentralize, cooperative	vs.	Top-down centralized
Labor relations	Considerate , diplomatic	vs.	Conflictual, unilateral
Communication	High level of details	vs.	Short, minimum information direct
Individuality	Group/teamwork, organization important	vs.	Individualized
Time orientation	Flexible, no pressure	vs.	Defined, rapid
Ownership	Public	vs.	Private
Management approach	Engineering, process, harmony	vs.	Financial, costs
Worker union	Yes	vs.	No

Another point that should be noted is the priorities of certain beliefs. Even if organizations have similar beliefs, and therefore would seem that they have a similar management culture, it is necessary to examine whether the emphases of the beliefs are different. Different emphases and priorities indicate, in essence, different beliefs regarding the priorities and therefore a difference, sometimes essential, in the management culture. For example, in many organizations, the managements ascribe importance to discipline in the organization. However, Intel is one of the only organizations that until recently noted discipline at the top of its priorities.

Measurement and Evaluation of Cultural Differences

The principles of measurement and evaluation of culture differences in M&As will be described here in short. It is necessary to remember that part of the planning process includes the evaluation of culture differences that is undertaken beforehand, or during, the negotiations process. In other words, it is necessary to at least perform the evaluation, if not the measurement, of cultural differences before the due diligence process in which it is possible to perform a precise measurement. This type of evaluation is the topic here.

Evaluation of culture and differences in culture is a complicated task. The methods can be based on direct and indirect contact with the target company to be acquired. When there is considerable contact with the target company, it is possible to use primary sources of information that are from the company itself. When there is no contact with the target company, or very little contact, then reliance is placed on secondary sources of information outside of the company.

In the planning process, reliance is primarily placed on secondary sources of information on the company. There are organizations in which such information about competitors, suppliers, and important clients is collected regularly in the framework of business intelligence.

In any event, you can collect information *ad hoc* from the following sources of information:

- Information published by the company—This information portrays its characteristics, such as its credo and its mission statement. In addition, this information can include the company's presentation on its website and press releases.

- Articles and interviews in the press—Interviews with senior managers from which the management approaches of the organization can be understood and, in addition, articles that review the organization in different business newspapers. Some newspapers methodically collect articles about many companies in the economy.

- Lectures and speeches given in different places by members of the management.

- Research divisions of different organizations collect material on many companies and the sectors in which they operate.

- Interviews with managers and workers in your organization who worked or who had a business relationship with the target company.

- Conversations and interviews with information holders, such as accountants, lawyers, management consultants, investment bankers, and so on, all of whom were in contact with the managers of the target company.

- Conversations with the managers and the workers of the target company at different events and encounters, such as study days, exhibitions, shared learning at a university, and so on.

For a public company, you can examine the company's financial reports, where there generally are announcements from the CEO to the stockholders. These announcements can add information about the organizational culture. There is interesting information in the company's material when the company recruits capital.

The evaluation of the culture and the differences will be undertaken on the basis of the dimensions of the culture and the additional areas of activity described previously. Thus, the evaluation of the culture can be performed methodically in a way that ranks the target company in its different dimensions. The collected information can be cross-checked to create reliability and examined against other topics to obtain validity. Furthermore, you can achieve the ranking using two or three scales and to examine the reliability of the ranking in its dimensions among the different scales. Obviously, the ranking requires considerable skill or at least initial support and aid.

The collection of the information also needs to be performed in the framework of the negotiation contracts. As described in Chapter 8, "Selection of Target and Negotiation Process," the negotiations should be held by a team. The team members should have simple training before the negotiations. Each one can collect information and even rank the evaluation of the target company's culture or the cultural differences in its dimensions and areas of activity, as described earlier. The collection of information in the negotiations process in the topic of management culture can be described as follows:

- Questions prepared beforehand, during the preparations for negotiations, on the different management approaches, and focused on the dimensions described previously.

- Direct questions on the characteristics of the other company's management culture.

- Observation of behaviors, ceremonies, and language of the other team in the negotiations.

- Reference to different topics that arise in the negotiation discussions and related to the company's mode of activity. For example, the manner of reference to the use of loans and outside capital, the importance ascribed to investments in R&D, the way in which behaviors and performances are rewarded, the organizational structure, the delegation of authorities, and the degree of formality in the processes of decision making, and so on.

- Request for different documents from the target company, when these documents indicate the management style, way of thinking, and other characteristics.

To recap, the information collected by the team members for the negotiations must be coded, ranked, and examined for purposes of reliability among the team members and cross-checked against information gathered from other sources.

Using Cultural Differences Analysis in All M&A Stages

The analysis of culture differences should be used in all stages of an M&A: planning, negotiations, and the integration of the organizations (refer to Table 6.2). For example, during the stage of planning, the degree of cultural differences of the different dimensions serves as an indication of future problems and challenges to be anticipated, and cost associated, during the PMI process.

Table 6.2   The Use of Corporate Cultural Differences Measurement at Different Stages of Mergers and Acquisitions

Stage 1: Planning

1. **Analysis of Cultural Differences**

   - Identification, assessment, and measurement of the organization's corporate culture dimensions

   - Comparing of several options for the M&A: characterization of the corporate cultures of the firms that are candidates for the M&A

   - Screening candidates for the M&A

   - Evaluation of the corporate cultural differences between the organization and the firm that is a can didate for the M&A:

     ○ Strength of the cultural differences

     ○ Areas of cultural differences (risk, decision-making processes, rewards, and so on)

     ○ Cultural differences in various functions (logistics, production, marketing, R&D, and so on)

2. **Analysis of Future Challenges During PMI and Synergy Realization**

   - Assess the implementation challenges, such as human resources problems and the turnover of key talents and top executives.

   - Recommend post-acquisition integration approach (preservation, absorption, and symbiosis) based on cultural differences.

   - Consider staffing and recruitment vis-à-vis culture clash.

   - Consider milestones and time required for integration of the organizations after the agreement.

   - Based on cultural challenges, examine the degree to which the synergy potential will be exploited after the merger (in marketing, R&D, collaborations, and so on).

3. **Financial Assessments**

   - Costs and expenses required for PMI process due to cultural differences

   - Level of productivity and revenues due to cultural differences effects during PMI process

   - Implication of culture clash for cash flow and on the value of acquisition

   - Expected impact on Earning per share (EPS) in different types of financing (loan and payment in stock)

Stage 2: Negotiations

1. **Preparation for Negotiations**

   - Assess the obstacles in communication following differences in management culture.

   - Plan and train managers for negotiations (strategies, tactics, red lines, and so on).

   - Identify, locate, and confirm for analysis of the cultural differences in the framework of the negotiations process.

   - Use cultural differences to negotiate value and payments of the M&A. Set the maximum price ("walk-away " price).

   - Include conditions in agreement such as level of turnover of key talents, and use this and other cultural issues for setting the modes, level, and number of payments (cash and shares).

   - Set the payments according to overcoming cultural effects during integration progress.

2. **Negotiations Stage**

   - Use cultural differences for the creation of appropriate atmosphere.

   - Introduce and discuss cultural differences and implementation difficulties anticipated for the achievement of the negotiations objective.

   - Prepare for interviews and assess the cultural differences during due diligence within the limits of knowledge, speed, and confidentiality.

3. **Signing of the Contract**

   - Set value of the acquisition while taking into account cultural differences and implementation difficulties.

   - Make sure that the plan and cooperation options are considered based on cultural differences.

   - Set the level and number of payments on the basis of progress and key milestones during PMI process.

   - Determine the price before a change of share value after the agreement.

Stage 3: Post-Acquisition Integration Process

1. Choose the appropriate post-acquisition integration approach.

2. Choose divisions, departments, and units for integration with focus on

   - Strength of the differences

   - Type of the differences

   - Functions of the differences (marketing and R&D)

3. Define the desired cultural integration.

4. Set criteria for success of cultural integration.

5. Create the control and evaluation system for assessing progress in the cultural integration.

During the negotiation process, incumbent executives must be ready to assess cultural differences to identify expected difficulties in communication caused by differences in corporate culture. Comprehending the challenges of implementation is likely to impact the maximum price to be paid and the mode of payment, given the expected complexities at the PMI process. During the integration stage, evaluating the type and strength of cultural differences can determine the choice of units that are to be integrated during the early or late stages of the process. Finally, measurable values of management culture and cultural differences enable better control, supervision, and feedback that are necessary for attaining the M&A deal's objectives.

Conclusion

The aim of this chapter is to foster the use and implementation of cultural difference assessment and measurements in all stages of M&As. This chapter emphasizes that evaluating and measuring cultural differences is essential in making the choice of the right partner for an M&A and should be examined and measured during both pre-merger planning and negotiation stages.

References

Gomes, E., Weber, Y., Brown, C., and Tarba, S.Y. (2011). *Mergers, acquisitions and strategic alliances: Understanding the process*. USA & UK: Palgrave Macmillan.

Hofstede, G. 1980. *Culture's consequences*. New-York: Sage.

Maltz, J. (2003). Bridging the cultural divide. *Globes*, (November 19).

7

SEARCHING, SCREENING, AND SELECTION OF M&A ALTERNATIVES

The potential acquirer who operated according to the knowledge and guidelines presented in the previous chapters is now ready to begin a process to search for a company to acquire. This process is the combination of methodical strategic planning and a matter of luck, namely to be in the right place at the right time. Those are not contrary; in essence, the ability to be in the right place at the right time is in most cases the result of planning and detailed work.

You must differentiate between the initial process of searching and screening organizations that are candidates for the M&A, and evaluating candidates, which lasts to the closing of the deal. Searching and screening includes criteria based on the design of the organization's strategy and objectives, the screening of candidates, knowledge creation of external factors, and initial contact with candidates for acquisition. This is all described in this chapter. The evaluation includes topics of negotiations, valuation, and due diligence, which are the topics of the next chapter.

The Process of Search and Identification

The process of search includes three primary steps. The first step is determining the criteria for the search and screening process. The second step is determining the search strategy. The third step, which is undertaken after the initial process of screening and classification, is the first approach to the candidates and the possibility of continuing the process. Before these steps, you must establish an M&A team or a unit for business development that can encourage a proactive approach to acquisitions and accumulate experience and knowledge in this complex domain of management.

Establishment of a Business Development Unit

The process of identifying and screening companies for an acquisition is performed for several business reasons, but in many cases it is an *ad hoc* process or a process with the goal of justifying a decision that has already been made. In these cases, the list of criteria is more suited to a company that has been identified and less suited to other alternatives. The approach is in many cases based on an emergent "opportunity," while the suitability to the company's strategic and operational needs is not clarified. This, of course, is a process that illustrates a nonsuitable approach to the implementation of organizational strategy. Therefore, in many cases, the stockholders, directors, and managers do not support such a project because they are not convinced that this is the appropriate alternative for the organization's needs (as in the merger of HP and Compaq). In contrast, when the acquisition underwent a process of fundamental search and screening, even the opponents were convinced of the value of the recommendation and eventually supported it.

The responsibility for identifying and screening candidates for acquisition is that of a business development unit or an M&A team. In relatively large organizations, there is a division that has this task as its main function—in other words, identifying and screening companies for acquisition is a "hunt" for transactions that can help the company close strategic and operational gaps and enable the organization's strategy implementation. In many cases, the business development unit needs to help the organization to achieve competitive advantages through the M&A before other competitors or struggle with them over a specific target.

The team involved in the pre-agreement process should be composed of personnel with complementary competencies and experiences (Gomes, E., Angwin, D., Weber, Y., and Tarba, S.Y. 2013), and choose the appropriate partner, not only for financial, managerial, or tax reasons, but also for strategic reasons such as to develop competitive capabilities and resources (Schweiger, D., Csiszar, E., and Napier, N. 1993). Based on data from more than 25 interviews with senior managers, investment bankers, and consultants, Jemison and Sitkin (1986) arrived at the conclusion that, despite the benefits of getting external advisors involved (given the complexity of the process), it is vital that the in-house top management gets fully involved and coordinates the entire process. Two main reasons were stated: i) The management needs to integrate a variety of specialized and fragmented views from the external consultants and ii) They need to combine the strategic fit analysis from external advisors (usually based on quantitative analysis) with more subtle and qualitative concerns related to the organizational fit of the companies.

Creating units and special teams can help the company to accumulate knowledge that can be applied to future cases. Another way of addressing the problem of integrating perspectives and getting a more balanced analysis (covering both financial and operational aspects) is by involving operations managers from an early stage of the pre-agreement process (Leighton, C. and Tod, R. 1969; Jemison, D. and Sitkin, S. 1986; Jeris,

L., Johnson, J. and Anthony, C. 2002). Their experience can help the team involved in the process to pay special attention to potential operating problems that analysts who lack a focus on operational processes might underestimate. Jemison and Sitkin (1986) provide the example of Sam Ginn, vice chairman of the Pacific Telesis Group, who always involves the operations manager who would be responsible for the new subsidiary, with the objective of bringing more hands-on realism to the merger analysis.

The tasks of the business development unit or of the M&A unit are critical to the success of the process of search and screening, which ends when the appropriate company for the merger is found—a main factor in the success of M&As. This unit/team has a number of important roles: encouraging a proactive approach to M&As, creating a center for search and screening of offers, and encouraging learning and accumulating knowledge. These roles are discussed next.

Encouragement of a Proactive Approach to M&As

Unit and operations managers are accustomed to developing their businesses from independent activities and not necessarily relying on the development based on M&As. They are also busy with competition and industry problem solving and the complicated engagement in the M&A is difficult for them. A business development unit specializing in this topic enables the managers to think about the activity of M&As knowing that they will have professional support elsewhere in the organization. In general, the encouragement of proactive thinking is important to every organization and in this case enables the search for M&As instead of waiting for things to occur. A business development unit specializing in an M&A also allows thoughts on complex mergers or acquisition of companies within a number of fields, knowing that there is somebody to deal with this complexity. For instance, if only part of a target is of interest to acquire, the business development unit can also address the divesture of the units that do not interest the company after the acquisition. Lastly, the experience of companies that have established business development units indicates that the organization can address many offers of M&As, and the process of search and screening brings offers for better mergers.

Center for Searching and Screening Offers

A whole industry of agents in the topic of M&As, such as investment bankers, engages in submitting offers to every party that appears to have an interest. However, these agents can find it difficult to guess or learn the strategic needs of organizations and the suitability of offers to these organizations. The unit for business development has that knowledge and serves as a focus point for all offers and contacts with outside parties. This unit can guide external and internal parties regarding what M&As are of interest.

Encouragement of Learning and Knowledge Accumulation

M&As are one of the most complex management operations, and thus a learning process based on organizational experience is required. The experience accumulated from acquisitions will be used in future acquisitions in the same organization and transferred between M&As. In essence, a post-acquisition analysis should be performed for every M&A—success or failure—also in those cases, the negotiations did not lead to any transaction. Effective drawing of conclusions will ask whether the results derive from certain managers, organizational systems and processes, changes in the industry, or a combination of such factors.

In the establishment of the unit for business development, it is necessary to think about the team size, the competencies, and the areas of work that will be included therein, as well as its position in the organization in terms of authorities and reporting. Generally, the unit will include a small number of skilled people. For example, in the Electrolux Company, which became the largest company in the world in sales of consumer durables following hundreds of M&As, one person dealt with an average of 25 completed acquisitions, 8 divestures of businesses, 10 uncompleted acquisitions, and approximately 120 evaluations of potential acquisitions per year.

The people on the M&A team include, in addition to the business unit manager(s), lawyers, accountants, finance persons, and outside expert consultants on the matter of M&As. Every one of these professionals can be recruited temporarily for each merger offer from inside or outside the organization. Lastly, it is important that the unit reports to the most senior management in the company and to those directly under the CEO. The direct and immediate relationship can be critical in cases in which speed is necessary, such as the need to meet the deadlines of a tender for the acquisition of a company. Therefore, in certain cases, it is necessary to enable an immediate contact, in coordination with the CEO, with two to three board members, as well, to obtain initial commitment to the process.

Determination of Criteria for the Search and Screening

The organization's strategy is the starting point for all the activities of the business development unit. It provides a clear definition of the organization's vision, mission, and goals. The people in the unit must know the organization's strategy well—in many cases, they are partners in the process of designing the vision, mission, and goals. In essence, the process of strategic planning already addresses the competitive advantages and competencies that the organization will develop in internal processes as opposed to those that it will achieve using M&As. The growth rate and profitability that also link to organic growth vis-à-vis M&As are also defined in the organization's strategy. For example, Teva has the objective of doubling sales every 4-5 years, in part through organic growth and in part through acquisitions. The business development unit first performs a strategic and operational gap analysis that leads to the initial criteria for search and screening. The results of this analysis are described in Tables 7.1 and 7.2.

The first column in Table 7.1 refers to the strategic factors of interest for the management team. For each of these factors, there might be a strategic gap that the management aspires to reduce or close through a merger or acquisition. For instance, strategic topics such as the need to extend areas of competencies and skills, the acquisition of technological know-how, the adding of new market segments, control over distribution channels, acquisition of additional competitive advantages, and so on can be the topics that appear in the table. In the second column, the present situation (extant situation) is described, and in the third column, the aspirational situation is detailed. The difference between the second and the third columns is described in the fourth column as the existing strategic gap. The fifth column presents the ranking of importance and preference from a strategic perspective; in other words, what is the importance of the gap and urgency of reducing the gap. The last column describes the contribution of the closing of the entire strategic gap. For instance, the extension of the areas of engagement enables the reduction of risk, the increase of growth, and the increase of profitability following possible synergies between the existing and new areas of engagement. The increase of the market share enables the increase of profitability following the reduction of costs due to advantage of size, which derives from the bargaining power versus suppliers and the possibility to buy larger volumes at better prices. This reduction of costs also can be used to improve the competitive advantage and increase sales.

Table 7.1   Analysis of Strategic Gaps

Strategic Factors	Present Situation	Desired Situation	Strategic Gap	Ranking of Importance	Advantages of Reducing/ Closing the Gap through M&As
Areas of engagement					
Rates of growth and profitability					
Technological abilities					
Market segments, shares					
Development of markets in new geographic areas					
Levels of product differentiation					

Strategic Factors	Present Situation	Desired Situation	Strategic Gap	Ranking of Importance	Advantages of Reducing/ Closing the Gap through M&As
Competitive advantages					
Distribution channels					
Structure of costs					
Management culture					
Management abilities					
Others					

The conclusions of this table indicate the industry, business, and organization in which the company will have the most interest and constitute an important step in the search and screening process. For example, an organization interested in increasing its market shares and adding additional market segments can focus on the industry in which it operates and acquire competitors and companies with complementary products or services. If the organization sees opportunities in the development of new geographic markets, one of the first criteria leads to the search for companies to acquire in these new geographic areas. The Finnish software developer BasWare's acquisition of Swedish Momentum Doc exemplifies this. If again the organization is interested in extending its competence area, acquiring a company according to its target area would provide a solution. Teva was, for instance, interested in extending its activity in the injectable field and therefore acquired the Dutch company Pharmachemie. A company could also be interested in dealing with threats and challenges in the area of distribution and would therefore focus its acquisition efforts on finding companies in the industry in which companies engaging in distribution operate. Electra acquired some ownership of Sensor and Shekem to promote the distribution of its consumption products, for instance. The acquisition of distribution channels or suppliers is called *vertical acquisition*, whereas the acquisition of competitors or manufacturers of complementary products is called *horizontal acquisition*.

In other words, the analysis of strategic gaps defines the first search and screening criterion: the industry or industries of a potential target. This criterion is based on the organization's strategic needs and defines the abilities that the company is interested in finding in the acquired company. These abilities are part of the second analysis: the analysis of operational gaps. If, for instance, there is an interest in integrating forward and acquiring distribution channels, then the acquired company will have appropriate distribution abilities that include appropriate deployment, appropriate distribution capacity, suitable clients, and so on that actually fit with the acquirer's capabilities.

Analysis of the operational gaps defines in detail the operational needs of the organization in the different functions. In Table 7.2, the first column addresses the organization's areas of operations and includes a list of processes, skills, and abilities in which the organization is interested. The second and third columns, like in Table 7.1, describe the present situation and the desired situation, while the fourth column describes the gap. The fifth column emphasizes the ranking of importance of the gap in each area from the organization's perspective. The sixth column describes the advantages of closing the gap.

Table 7.2   Analysis of the Operational Gaps

Primary Operational Elements	Present Situation	Desired Situation	Strategic Gap	Ranking of Importance	Advantages of Reducing/ Closing the Gap through M&As
Manufacturing Equipment Processes					
Marketing Salesperson's skills Research and marketing understanding ability Access to market segments Distribution abilities					

Primary Operational Elements	Present Situation	Desired Situation	Strategic Gap	Ranking of Importance	Advantages of Reducing/ Closing the Gap through M&As
Research and Development Development ability Speed to market					
Human Resources Management ability Reward and motivation systems Organizational culture					
Finance Level of profitability Tax considerations Level of cash flows					
Other Topics					

The analysis of strategic and operational gaps results in the identification of the characteristics of the ideal target company's profile that complements the organization's strategic and operational needs. The business development team will develop the criteria for the search and screening on the basis of this analysis. Obviously, the criteria will be ranked by order of priority. The top criteria for the search are also the *deal breakers* in terms of determining the candidates. Generally, these criteria will be

- The industry of interest (distributor, supplier, and competitor)

- The company size (for instance, the level of sales)
- The initial asking price (which might indicate a price that is out of reach for the investment determined in the organization)

Other criteria that might be deal breakers are defined by the company according to its needs, such as:

- **The level of profitability**—Some companies do not want to engage and invest time in the management of the acquired company to make it profitable; others might acquire firms for exactly that reason.

- **Differences of organizational culture**—The acquiring company will want to avoid implementation problems and difficulty in the exploitation of the potential of synergies and will prefer a low level of cultural differences.

- **Level of synergy**—Requirement for high level of synergies that will ensure high profitability after covering the merger expenses.

The choice of the criteria will be based on the management's needs. Through combining different criteria into an acquisition matrix, such as the one depicted in Table 7.3, you can weight the impact of different effects against one another and thereby determine their overall impact, rather than their separate effects. The contribution of synergies and the additional financial advantages (such as tax advantages) are examined here versus difficulties of implementation (in terms of the differences of organizational culture). This matrix describes four situations, and in each cell of the matrix, there is a recommendation for action.

Table 7.3   Screening of Candidates for Acquisition Matrix: Implementation Difficulties

		Synergy and Financial Advantages	
		Few	Many
Implementation Difficulties	Many	Not interesting for acquisition	Requires in-depth and cautious examination
Cultural Differences	Few	Depends on alternatives and personal approach to risk	Preferred for aquisition

The use of different criteria, which are developed on the basis of the strategic and operational analysis of the organization, is the difference between professional search and screening and the amateurish process based only on opportunities. In essence, the list of criteria enables a mini-due diligence to be performed in the initial stages of the process and thus facilitates the process of screening before further resources are invested in the examination processes.

Determination of Search Strategy

To begin the search process, you must prepare the following:

- List of *criteria* that characterize the target company and that is based on the organization's chosen strategy as detailed here and in the previous chapters.

- Definition of the *investments budget* that is aimed at the acquisition and that will help in the initial process of screening for candidates. The budget can be flexible in case of special opportunities and can include payment in stocks in addition to cash.

- Information on the *price* that is paid for similar targets in the industry that interest the acquirer. The manner of payment in the industry and the parameters for the determination of the price, such as ratio of the price to the company value according to its stocks, and so on are important.

Now the acquirer can begin to search or can integrate with an independent search with the help of agents. Experience shows that the sole reliance on different agents (such as investment bankers, accountant officers, and so on) is far from adequate. The frequent disappointment among acquirers with these agents is expressed in statements such as "They don't understand my business and my needs, and their offers do not contain enough information or analysis." The other side of that story is that the different agents often complain about their clients: "The clients want to see every possible transaction; otherwise, they think that they have lost an opportunity. They complain about every transaction that I show them—it is not suitable or it is too expensive. I don't understand what interests them. It seems to me that they don't know what they want."

The best way to avoid these conflicts is to develop a process of independent search in which offers from agents are incorporated as necessary. In the process, the organization will appoint a person or unit, who engages in the search and screening and is not dependent on agents. In addition, in the independent search, the organization develops criteria for screening and even accumulates experience in screening so that it guides the agents instead of being guided by them.

Independent Search Plan

The independent search plan is based on the organization's strategic analysis and strategic needs and on criteria derived from the analysis of the operational and strategic gaps. The next step is identifying the candidates for acquisition according to the industry, or industries, that the acquirer defined. Generally, these are industries related to the acquirer's activities. In other words, the acquirer examines companies for acquisition from among its competitors and might also consider companies with complementary products. If the acquirer examines the possibilities of upstream vertical acquisitions (acquisitions of companies at preceding positions in the supply chain; backward integration), the examination can focus on the suppliers and manufacturers of raw materials and machinery, and transportation with which the acquirer has relations. If the acquirer examines the possibilities of downstream vertical acquisition (acquisitions of companies at positions later in the supply chain; forward integration), it examines distributors and companies that provide maintenance services for its products, and even marketing research and information companies, when these are critical for success.

The collection of information on these companies and on others begins with accessible public information based on stock market data and university databases, newspapers, data from different authorities, and information provided from companies against payment, such as BDI and D&B. Semiformal information can be obtained from different parties such as analysts and research divisions of banks. Informal information can be collected from consultants, including lawyers, accountants, sales personnel, purchasers, and other management consultants. In addition, the people of the organization who are found in direct and indirect contact with clients, competitors, and suppliers can provide important information after they receive appropriate directives. The Internet further allows for the relatively easily obtained information on foreign firms through information bases found abroad. If confidentiality is not a main problem, it is possible to release an announcement in the business press on the interest in acquiring a company in a certain industry and to cite the appropriate size range. This type of advertisement can lead to many answers, but many of them will not be suitable.

The list of candidates that arises from these sources is not complete. Remember that most of the information is not entirely precise or up-to-date. In addition, it would not include the many relatively small firms, privately owned firms, or recently established start-up companies. In essence, advanced stages of the search recall detective work in which details are collected from different sources and cross-examined in a process of business intelligence.

Search through Agents

After all these steps, the acquiring party is now ready to enter into the lions' den of the investment bankers, business agents, and firms interested in being sold. It is often enough for large firms interested in making an acquisition deal to give a hint about this to others, to then be approached with offers. Large firms are often courted with offers and ideas for acquisitions by different investment bankers and agents. Small firms, which are of less interest to the major investment bankers, can turn to small agents or to their accountant and lawyer. Obviously, it is possible to also turn to bankers, companies that engage in the valuation of firms, and management consultants that engage in M&As. It might be worthwhile to obtain services from a third party that is not an investment banker but another professional agent or expert on M&As. This is especially true for medium-sized or small companies. An investment banker invests in the learning about the organization, prepares many documents, and helps with the evaluation of the worth, negotiations, financing, and so on. Because of this high overhead, the costs are high. Conversely, some agents assist only in making the acquaintance between the acquiring and the acquired companies. Between these two poles, there are parties providing different levels of service. For instance, different management consultants with experience in M&As can provide, at relatively low costs, initial value assessments, which are not necessarily exact but do define the possible range of prices well. People with this experience can help in the negotiations process. Thus, you can save costs and considerable amounts of time that is usually required for screening offers that are not necessarily relevant to the company.

In large firms, primarily those interested in several acquisitions, a unit should be appointed because of the aforementioned reasons. In any event, firms of different sizes can turn to professional agents and even hire private consultants who can help in the different stages, both with the other company and with the professional agents. The costs would depend on the execution of the transaction, the receipt of services such as assessment of the value, negotiations, or a combination of the two. A method for calculation of payment is, for example, the 1-2-3 method (for example, the payment is 3 percent of the sum obtained up to 10 million dollars, an additional 2 percent of the sum obtained between 10 and 15 million dollars, and additionally 1 percent of the sum obtained above 15 million dollars; payments describing those of the divesting firm). Obviously, other possibilities are also acceptable, such as a fixed price and additional sums for defined services.

The agreement between the company and the consulting party also addresses other points, such as:

- Does the consultant have exclusivity in the finding of a company? Generally, the company will not be interested in this situation so that it retains its freedom of action.

- Does the consultant help in other areas such as the assessment of value, negotiations, preparation of reports, and so on?

- Is there a commitment to preserve confidentiality?

- Under what conditions is the agreement terminated?

Approaching the Target Company

You can divide the different approaches to the target company in three ways:

- Friendly approach

- A making-the-most-of-the-opportunity approach

- Hostile approach

Friendly Approach

This approach is normally directed at the senior management, and the idea of the possibility of an M&A is presented. This approach is generally characterized by relatively low costs in terms of time and money. Another characteristic is that the acquired management remains following the acquisition, and the acquirer has a laid-back approach to the information of the acquired company.

Despite the friendly approach, the CEO of the acquired company might have fears of losing power and authority. The success of this approach depends on the interpersonal communication abilities of the acquiring company's CEO—especially with the CEO of the company to be acquired. In addition, when the approach develops into negotiations, the proposed price needs to be attractive from the beginning. The CEO of the company that is a candidate for acquisition will greatly want to maintain confidentiality, especially in a public company because the rumors can cause fluctuations in the stock price. In any case, if the negotiations do not bear fruit in an M&A, the stockholders will be concerned and the CEO will be in an uncomfortable position.

Making-the-Most-of-the-Opportunity Approach

This approach addresses the situation in which it is known that the target company is a candidate for acquisition following such an announcement on its part or information from agents such as investment banks. It might also be the case that the information is out that the target company is a candidate for a hostile takeover by another firm. In this case, it is easy to approach the target company as the "knight in shining armor." As late as the target has agreed to the acquisition, you can approach it in a friendly manner and create a situation of a tender, which is convenient for the acquired company. You must take into consideration time constraints and special requirements of the acquired company, including nonfinancial demands, to meet the tender conditions.

The making-the-most-of-the-opportunity approach further includes acquiring firms based to "bargain" prices. This would include buying a firm that is in financial need to be acquired but has found it difficult to find an appropriate acquirer. Or it may include the acquisition of family-owned firms when the next generation does not show any interest in taking over the firm or is lacking. What is a bargain is of course problematic to say in advance but would generally follow from how good the company is at generating profit and thereby the return on investment for the acquirer.

Hostile Approach

This refers to the attempt to perform a hostile takeover of the target company. Generally, the approach is directed to the stockholders, while bypassing the target firm's management, because the management would object to the acquisition. In this case, the costs are high because the price offer is generally higher than the traded stock price. In addition, the price of the company's stocks generally rises greatly within a short period of time. Conversely, there is the possibility to acquire a relatively small percentage of the company's stocks without the threats of takeover and only then to propose the acquisition of the remainder of the stocks. In this case, the rise of the stock value in a short period of time enables the potential acquiring company to offer the stocks it has already bought at a relatively high price to the target company or to another "knight in shining armor." When the Swedish truck company BT Industries acquired its U.S. counterpart, Raymond, this was a process preceded by a company raid. Actors had started buying shares in Raymond and as these reached a certain level of ownership, they approached the board and requested a divestment of the company. From BT Industries' perspective, Raymond was a company that fit well into its strategic plans of geographical expansion and the management of BT Industries grasped this opportunity, however at a costly price for the Raymond shares.

Hostile takeovers were widespread in the United States in the 1980s. Now they are rarer, as a result of legislation, a high general fluctuation in stock prices which makes this a risky process, and the avoidance of banks and insurance companies from financing this type of transaction.

Do's and Do Not's

- Do Not: It is important not to skip the process of search, screening, and selection, which examines a number of alternatives.

- Do: Appoint a team or manager to dedicate most of its/his time to the search and screening of companies for acquisition. In the continuation, this team or manager will engage in the assimilation of the acquired organization.

- Do: Analyze every candidate for M&A according to criteria derived from the organization's strategic plan and from the analysis of strategic and operational gaps.

- Do Not: It is important not to rely only on external parties in the process of search and screening. Use an independent search plan as well.

References

Gomes, E., Angwin, D., Weber, Y., and Tarba, S.Y. (2013). Critical success factors through the mergers and acquisitions process: Revealing pre- and post-M&A connections for improved performance. *Thunderbird International Business Review*, 55 (1), 13-35.

Leighton, C. and Tod, R. (1969). After the acquisition: continuing challenge. *Harvard Business Review*, March–April, 90–102; Jemison, D. and Sitkin, S. (1986). The process can be a problem. *Harvard Business Review*, 107–116; Jeris, L., Johnson, J. and Anthony, C. (2002). HRD involvement in merger and acquisition decisions and strategy development: four organizational portraits. *International Journal of Training and Development*, 6, 1: 2–12.

Schweiger, D., Csiszar, E., and Napier, N. (1993). Implementing international mergers and acquisitions. *Human Resource Planning*, 16, 1: 53–70.

PART III

Negotiation

8

SELECTION OF TARGET
AND NEGOTIATION
PROCESS

The previous chapter discussed the selection and scanning process for candidates to acquire. This chapter covers some of the key issues related to negotiation, the choice of the partner, and the evaluation of the contribution that each partner can make to the combined venture.

In the negotiation for a merger or acquisition, the acquirer makes deals with the divesting party. Such deal-making can include intense price negotiations, in which the acquirer might pay a premium for the acquired party. There is also the issue of information asymmetry between the divesting party and the acquirer, which means that the acquirer negotiates from an inferior position in terms of knowledge on the target. Consequently, the acquirer might find unpleasant surprises after taking over the target company. The acquirer might be willing to pay a premium for the target firm, based on synergies between the acquirer and that firm, or even as a means to keep competitors away from reaching the target company. Although the former motive to pay a premium is expected to be covered through cost-savings, the latter aspect becomes more troublesome in that regard.

Figure 8.1 depicts the negotiation process of an M&A and constitutes the basis for this chapter. As can be seen in the figure, the process of negotiation should be based on the motives of the deal and the defined strategy and goals to be achieved. These various steps have already been discussed in the previous chapter, therefore, this chapter focuses on the process of negotiating an M&A agreement including choice of partner, evaluation of partner, price valuation, negotiation, and closing the deal.

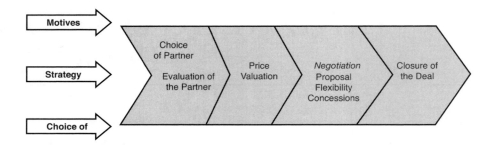

Figure 8.1   The process of negotiating an M&A agreement

Choice of Partner

As described in the previous chapter, there are two principal ways in which potential acquisition opportunities are identified. Either the company is approached to express interest when a business is marketed for sale (*opportunistic*), or it actively seeks acquisition opportunities (*strategic*). Ideally, the same approach of screening should be applied for both opportunistic deals and strategic ones. A key challenge in assessing potential acquisitions is to balance the need to think strategically with the need to react opportunistically, often with tight timelines. To assist in this process, the development business unit must define screening criteria adapted to the strategy of the firm. As pointed to, these screening criteria are designed to serve a number of purposes:

- They reinforce and clarify the strategic message by clearly defining what specific attributes and capabilities the organization is looking to acquire and how these can help the company to achieve the business goals.

- They define the levels of financial performance expected from the target company.

- They assist in weeding out deals that might be politically or emotionally motivated.

- They enable deals that have a low probability of success to be terminated as early as possible so that resources can be focused on assessing and targeting appropriate opportunities. This saves both time and money and can assist in more rapid delivery of the strategic goal fulfillment.

It is envisaged that screening will be done at a number of levels—moving from high-level screening to more specific, fine-grade screening. Screening will typically be related to strategic, financial, or deal achievability (see Table 8.1). In simple terms, this process looks at multiple companies that broadly meet the profile of what the acquirer is after and then passes them through increasingly detailed screening/filters to come up with a short list of target companies. After this short list is established, further work is done with regard to the more detailed profiling of the short-listed companies and the selection of the preferred targets.

Table 8.1   High Level M&A Screening

Strategic	Financial	Achievability
Market access	Size	Regulatory
• Geography	Growth	Management style
• Product	Margins	Unions
• Customer	ROCE	Organization culture
• Speed to market	Synergies	Ownership structure
Capability access		Risk profile
Opportunity to access value		
Scale		
• Market power		
• Scale economies		
• Speed to scale		

Under these areas, there will be screen-out criteria (that is, factors that would make a target undesirable) and screen-in criteria (factors that would make a target desirable). Examples of screening-in and out criteria are detailed in Table 8.2.

Table 8.2   Screen-In and Screen-Out Criteria

Screen-Out Criteria	Screen-In Criteria
No clear fit with approved strategy	Compelling solution that competitors (existing or potential) cannot match, and customers clearly see value of
No clear or compelling proposition	
Low growth, commodity, which offers limited ability to add value to the business through market knowledge, customer relationships, cost position, and so on	Clear connection between one or more existing customer relationships, technology, processes, or capabilities
No fit with capabilities, and/or competencies and/or standards	Opportunity for the company, their customers, and suppliers to benefit (revenue increase, cost decrease, and/or improved performance)
Scale of long-term opportunity not sufficient to outweigh start-up cost and effort	Opportunity for international/global rollout
No sustainable long-term value proposition	Capital-efficient
Insufficient ability to manage risk versus return	

This is not a complete list; other types of screening could include factors such as:

- Target revenue of at least £Xm or potential to achieve £Xm within 2 years
- Operating margins of Y percent
- Annual growth of Z percent
- Valuation of between £Am - £Bm
- Compatibility of management style, decision-making processes (for example, bureaucratic or entrepreneurial)
- Technology or processes that are patented
- Ability to achieve regulatory approvals
- Number 1 or 2 in market position
- Recognized as best-in-class technology
- Do-ability of deal based on ownership structure

The best screenings are those that filter out business opportunities with the greatest potential for success and the greatest ability to contribute to strategic goal fulfillment.

The screening criteria can be more or less important. Consideration should therefore be given to weight them. This also enables greater differentiation between similar targets. The time spent on screening can significantly reduce the time required to identify, assess, and select the targets. Because the targets have been qualified by going through a rigorous screening process, the probability that the deal will be successful increases. No screening process is watertight though, so you must maintain a common-sense approach that also picks up candidates that might incorrectly be rejected solely based on the criteria.

Sources of Information

To obtain the necessary information with which to both identify and screen potential targets, there are numerous possible sources of information, such as:

- Company employees (executive teams, sales teams, R&D group, and so on). An environment needs to be created so that employees are aware what the business is trying to achieve (understand strategy and key drivers of growth/value) and how they can contribute to the identification/screening efforts.

- Company databases (for example, Dun & Bradstreet, and Thompson Financial)

- Industry associations (member lists, conferences, monthly magazines, and researchers)

- Company websites

- Universities (research projects and leading professors)

- Newspaper/magazine searches and news desk services

- Trade journals and trade shows

- Customers and suppliers

- Competitors (publicly available information)

- Investment bankers and venture capital firms. These will be industry specialists that have a strong understanding for your particular target market.

- Broker reports (identify who follows which stock)
- Review of recent patents, trademark applications, and their approvals
- Freelance industry experts and consultants
- Market surveys

Gathering information should not be seen as an event that occurs once, but relationships should rather be developed that result in an ongoing feed of opportunities that are then reviewed against such screening criteria as previously discussed.

Another aspect that companies should take into consideration when choosing the potential target is size and power similarities. Research on strategic alliances points to such aspects in addition to the business relatedness of firms (Bleeke and Ernst's, 1991; Chung et al., 2000; Ahuja and Katila, 2001), while other findings point to inconclusiveness in these aspects and also to acquisitions. In the acquisition, a much bigger acquirer can be fruitful because available resources can then be deployed by the acquired party. The acquisitions of Jaguar and Land Rover by Ford and of Rover by BMW help to illustrate this point. The two cases in which a big company (Ford) acquired a much smaller company (first Jaguar and then Land Rover) were more successful than when the two companies of similar size merged (BMW/Rover). In the case of Jaguar, it took more than 10 years and 4 billion dollars of investment to turn it around. With Land Rover, Ford showed the same level of commitment and capacity of investment as it did with Jaguar. In contrast, after six consecutive years of losses, BMW decided to sell the Rover business. This indicates that the difference in size between BMW and Ford certainly played an important role. BMW did not have the same level of resources as Ford to endure the heavy burden it had been carrying for six years. Therefore, it can be argued that differences in the size of merging companies are not necessarily detrimental to merger performance. On the contrary, when the larger company handles the process with a great level of commitment, it can actually prove to be beneficial. This is the case in which the larger company can deploy its resources and competencies into the smaller one.

When a suitable target is chosen, then companies should undertake a more thorough analysis of the strategic, organizational, financial, and cultural aspects of the potential target. This includes the strategic fit and operational fit. These analyses will help in negotiation stages to evaluate the acquisition and discuss future obstacles for smooth implementation. Therefore, it is important that companies consider not only the hard factors (strategy, structures, and systems), but also the soft aspects of the potential partner: its culture, staff, management and business style, skills and goals.

Evaluation of the Target

Evaluation of Strengths and Weaknesses of the Target Company

Overestimating the strengths and weaknesses of the product or market position of the target has been indicated in the literature as a common mistake (Van de Vliet, 1997; Donnelly et al., 2001; Thompson, 2001; Angwin 2001; Gomes et al., 2008; Gomes et al., 2009). Successful companies have the ability to weight the strengths and weaknesses of potential target companies in a short period of time. This is complicated enough for domestic M&As but becomes even more difficult in international M&As because it requires a good understanding of differences in political, economic, legal, and cultural aspects. In cases in which companies want to make agreements in countries where they have no presence, it would be advisable to seek a local intermediary to assist in the process. Pritchett, Robinson, and Clarkson give an interesting illustration stating that a collaborative agreement is like buying a secondhand car: "We try to do our homework, but the pre-agreement analysis never tells us all we need to know…the other guy is going to highlight the positives while concealing or downplaying problems" (1997).

Evaluation of the Quality of the Target's Management Team

Another critical mistake that many companies make at this stage is overestimating the quality of the partner's management team, its core competencies, strategic capabilities, cultural and behavior patterns. Managers of the buying company interested in merging with another company need to have good links with various sources of intelligence to determine the real competencies, talent, and management style of the targeted company. Pritchett, Robinson, and Clarkson (1997) cite research done by Acquisitions Horizons evaluating 537 companies that made at least one acquisition within a 5-year time frame. The most frequently mentioned reason for unsuccessful results was that the management of the acquired company was not as strong as expected. They also state that in many cases, some of the key management talent left the firm after the merger.

Evaluation of Investment Requirements

A realistic and accurate estimation of the future investment requirements will be a major influence on the profitability of the M&A. Research evidence shows that there is a tendency to underestimate the investment in both financial and nonfinancial terms. Successful companies make a careful analysis of the future investment requirements. Kitching (1967) asserts that, even in the case of successful mergers, parent companies tend to underestimate their subsidiaries' future requirements for investment. An example of this was BMW's acquisition of Rover where the investment requirements were clearly underestimated, also resulting in a lower than estimated return on investment.

For M&As, when firms recognize a potential suitable partner and have the possibility to experiment with a "courtship period" before a definite deal, the merger implementation will be much more successful. This is because a courtship period gives the opportunity for partners to know each other better by cooperating in short-term common projects, and make an evaluation, not just based on the usual strategic and financial aspects but also on the more subtle cultural issues that ultimately tend to manifest during the implementation stage. Before acquiring Jaguar, Ford did not have a courtship period with the company. This fact, combined with its lack of experience and capacity in weighing the strengths and weaknesses of the target in a short period of time, strongly contributed to a poor evaluation process. In turn, this resulted in the overestimation of the Jaguar brand and the underestimation of the investment requirements. As a result, Ford ended up paying too high a premium for the acquisition (£1.6 billion). Conversely, Dyer, Kale, and Singh (2004) provide the example of a successful acquirer that consider the courtship period as a critical success factor. These authors argue that approximately 25 percent of the Cisco acquisitions started as small equity investments. They assert that this enabled Cisco to get some partners to accelerate development of products and evaluate firms to determine if acquisitions would work. According to the company, it takes between 12 and 18 months to build trust with partners and decide if the companies can work together. The equity relationships helped Cisco move quickly to prevent rivals and acquire firms when the time was right. Cisco has also used acquisitions and alliances successfully because it has developed processes that help it determine when to use which strategy (Dyer et al., 2004).

This provides evidence that companies who have an overall strategy for growth and accumulated experience on merger activity, and tend to establish a courtship period before the merger, will have more possibilities to plan in advance and choose the right form of arrangement and the right target, and be in a privileged position to make a much better evaluation of the company.

Price Valuation

After a careful and comprehensive evaluation of the future target, companies are in a better position to negotiate the right price. It is vital to make a good evaluation of the target and avoid paying too high a price. Jemison and Sitkin assert that "[t]he pressure to close the deal quickly can prevent managers from considering strategic and organizational fit issues completely and dispassionately and can lead to premature conclusions" (1986: 110). They suggest that the more managers identify with the agreement, the more difficult it becomes for them to consider it objectively and accept criticism that could slow or stop the process. Goold, Campbell, and Alexander (1994: 220) assert that "[o]ne of the most common and most important sources of value destruction in corporate development is paying too much. In the case of M&A, often the acquirer destroys value by paying too much, making it very difficult to achieve an adequate return." Van de Vliet, quoting Piers Whitehead, vice president at Mercer, says that this often happens because "[m]anagement falls in love with the deal once their egos are boosted for running bigger companies" (1997: 40).

The evaluation of targets in situations of cross-border acquisitions needs to be handled even more carefully because on average there is greater information asymmetry between companies from different countries than in domestic situations. Inkpen, Sundaram, and Rockwood (2000) analyzed all the technology-based merger activity involving U.S. companies that were the closest approximation to Silicon-Valley-type firms during the period of 1990 to 1999 and arrived at the conclusion that the failure rate of acquisitions involving European acquirers was much higher than those involving U.S. acquirers because European companies tended to pay a much higher premium (43 percent) than U.S. acquirers (14 percent).

Child and Faulkner (1998) argue that in the case of an M&A, the price is determined by the market, and there are other potential bidders that can enter the process, which makes the price more transparent than in, for instance, alliances. The resources and time spent in evaluating the target's contribution will vary according to the critical success factors of each particular industry. Child and Faulkner (1998) suggest that there are two main types of factors to be considered: i) hard factors, those that are easy to distinguish and are valued in accountability terms (fixed assets, working capital, and past and present profitability of the partner) and ii) soft factors such as intangible assets that are more difficult to measure but that can be critical to the success of a company. The soft factors such as brand names, expertise, contact network, and technology transfer are often the main motives for the M&A and alliances.

Negotiation

Opportunities for M&A failure often lie in the process of negotiations, which can be deficient in two areas: First, the creation of chemistry and an action plan may remain outside of the process. Second, most people who engage in the creation of the transaction—lawyers, accountants, investment bankers, and even M&A teams of many organizations—depart immediately with the closing of the deal, with no responsibility for the success of the implementation. The negotiation should, as much as possible, take place in a way that companies feel the agreed deal is positive for all parties. This is particularly important because the conclusion of the deal represents the beginning of a new stage in which companies will start working together. As shown in Figure 8.2, if both parties follow this principle, by not only trying to safeguard their own interests but also the interests of the other party, the overall outcome will certainly be more positive for both, and the merger will have more chances of success in the long term.

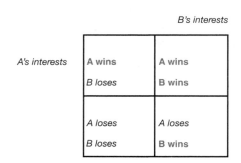

Figure 8.2   Possible negotiation outcomes (Fisher R., and Ury W. 1981)

Therefore, the win-win situation strongly depends upon the identification and pursuit of shared interests. This is one of the reasons why, as previously mentioned, mergers involving companies with status similarity in terms of size and power tend to be more successful. In addition, Fisher and Ury (1981) argue that a key ingredient to a successful negotiation process is the search for a solution that satisfies both sides' primary goals. They add that as a means to bring flexibility to the negotiation process, each party should negotiate based on objectives and alternatives and never on pre-established rigid positions. Therefore, it is recommended that companies come to the negotiation table with a range of alternative outcomes that they would be willing to accept. They must decide on the best (roof) and the worst (floor) possible deals. This can help a company to identify its BATNA (Best Alternative To a Negotiated Agreement) option and can clarify the strength of one's negotiating position, when compared with the other party's BATNA. Another important aspect that companies need to understand during negotiations is the cultural differences. This is especially the case in cross-border situations in which cultural differences are more marked. Managing cultural differences is a sensitive and critical aspect that needs the utmost attention from an early stage of the process when choosing, evaluating, and negotiating.

Stages in the Negotiations Process

Many stages in the M&A process can be performed in separate parts. In contrast, the stage of negotiations is an interactive process, with numerous iterations and many activities that are undertaken in parallel by a number of people on the merger/transaction team. According to the approach presented in this chapter, the goals of the negotiation should address, in addition to the transaction price, other aspects such as control, manner of organization management, and implementation of the post-agreement integration plan of the organizations. Weber (2003) describes four main steps in the negotiations process, and each one of them has secondary stages (see Figure 8.3). This is a comprehensive description, but in each case, there are stages that will be undertaken in a different order or will not be performed at all.

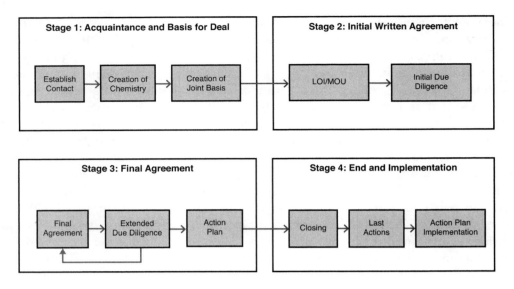

Figure 8.3   Stages in the negotiations process

The first stage is acquaintance and formation of the business basis, in which each party feels that it has benefitted from the transaction. In the second stage, there is a meaningful change in the business style, and in it there is an important formulation of the transaction principles. In the third stage, which includes in-depth examinations of the business (appropriate examinations and due diligence), there is formulation of the final agreement. It is greatly desired that an action plan that details the manner of degree of connection of the organizations (integration) will be made before this agreement is signed. Last, in the final stage, there is a process of closing the deal and activating the implementation plan.

Establish Contact

When the preferred target companies have been identified a Target Contact strategy needs to be developed. As the selling process effectively commences from the first contact, it is important that this is given the appropriate consideration. The following section describes a number of the key considerations and options in this stage of the acquisition process. Deals can be made or lost at this stage, so it is recommended that this is given appropriate consideration.

A range of the key considerations will include

1. Who should contact be made with? Principal shareholders; company CEO/managers; company's bankers/lawyers.

2. How should contact be made? Initial phone conversation; face-to-face meeting; letter.

3. Will you make a formal proposal, leave a written document?

4. Who should make the initial contact? The initial contact with the target company is important and can be undertaken through a variety of means and people: CEO; business unit manager; anonymously through an investment banker; person within the company with personal relationships with the target; person within the company with business relationships with the target (for example, sales manager).

5. What do you want to say?

6. What is the specific message you want to give? Benefits to seller; why it makes sense, identified issues; and how problems will be dealt with.

7. Will you provide documents for them; give a formal presentation; or is the initial meeting more of an informal chat?

8. When should contact be made? Impact of restructuring programs (want to realize benefits before selling); new CEO appointments (lack of willingness to sell); other takeover offers (is the company already in play?); economic cycle (impact on financial performance/position versus reluctance to sell at a low value); proximity to year end (issues regarding ability to get to see the key people).

9. If contact receives a favorable response, how do you propose to progress discussions?

10. If contact receives a negative response, what are your other options to progress this or other opportunities?

Many managers are not comfortable with the creation of direct contact for fear of getting a less than positive response. Nevertheless, many acquirers use this approach successfully. This is especially prominent in the acquisition of small- and medium-sized companies controlled by private owners. Some maintain that 20 percent of all businesses are *dormant sellers*, who are willing to consider reasonable offers but recoil from agents, tenders, or the advertisement of such a possibility in the industry because there are implications of the business's continued activity with the suppliers, clients, and so on. In these cases, the acquirer who directly and discreetly approaches the company has a considerable advantage. However, the acquirer needs to be ready to have his approach rejected 80 percent of the time. In addition, some managers think that approaching a potential divesting party puts them in a weak position during the negotiations. However, the negotiation positions depend on the manner in which the negotiations are conducted. Therefore, for those who correctly conduct the negotiations, the initial approaches do not raise or lower a thing.

The direct approach can be performed through a letter to the CEO or the owners of the company that is a candidate for the acquisition. The letter is phrased relatively ambiguously and describes the interest in the target company. The letter will note that a telephone call to the letter recipient is to be expected shortly. During the telephone conversation, you should be ready to discuss a wide range of options, including the possibility that the acquirer will buy part or most of the company. Thorough preparation before the telephone conversation is essential. It is desirable to prepare the conversation points in writing. You must reach the topic quickly but indirectly. Identify yourself, your position, your company, and your advantages. Display understanding of the activities of the business that is a candidate for acquisition, even without a contact, which has business advantages. In other words, the person needs to relatively quickly describe the advantages of the acquisition. Of course, it is necessary to listen well to the other party's responses. If the contact has the potential for continuation, then the alternative of an M&A should be discussed in a face-to-face meeting.

In case of rejection, contact should be maintained with a senior manager or with the owners of the company. The retention of the contact develops the relations and creates an environment of respect and reciprocal trust. An initial rejection over time becomes, in many cases, a successful merger transaction. Thus, it is possible to once in a while visit the company that is a candidate for acquisition or to once in a while send a brochure on the acquiring company to indicate its progress. In every such contact, the interest that the acquirer has in the acquisition of the company can be noted. If and when the target company's owner shows interest, then generally the ongoing contact gives the buyer priority over other potential competitors for the response time, relations of trust, and even the final price.

The Creation of Chemistry

Chemistry describes the quality of the relations between the people who act in the merger of organizations. Chemistry is a psychological contract that is more important than the written and legal documents. It is not concrete, but it is essential to the success of the merger process because it is the "glue" that connects the transaction partners together. Without chemistry, energies and trust in the merger are absent. In a situation of lack of chemistry, the merger will fail even if, strategically and operationally, it is the right merger.

The main basis for chemistry between the parties is the degree of trust that the parties have for one another. Trust exists when a person believes that the other party will do the right things strategically and operationally and relates to how interest in success is shared between the parties and how parties will keep promises, although they may not be explicitly stated in the contract.

However, the negotiations process entails many points that make it difficult to create trust. The business experience that many people have is that it is necessary to be cautious and to even be suspicious of the true intentions of the other party in the transaction. Thus, frequently when a negotiations process is to begin, each party is cautious in the disclosure of its true interests so that it will not be exploited and can succeed in "closing" the deal. At the same time, the parties attempt to discover what the other party actually wants. In other words, it is a process in which there are suspicions from the beginning. Both parties try to reveal as little information as possible at the same time as they try to accumulate information from the other party.

In addition to these factors, both parties discern that they tend to do business differently, with different emphases and priorities. In essence, every management has a different culture, and organizational cultural differences are often revealed already in the first meeting between the parties. Sometimes, these differences create communication problems between the parties and lead to lack of trust. Culture can influence the way in which persons perceive and approach certain key elements in the negotiating process. Knowledge of these cultural differences can help negotiators to better understand and interpret their counterpart's negotiating behavior and to find ways to bridge gaps created by cultural differences (Salacuse, 1998). Wherever it actually occurs, negotiation requires people to focus on a variety of important dynamics: communication, trust-building, cross-cultural perceptions, personalities, bargaining styles, and tactics such as crafting offers and counteroffers (Saorin-Iborra, 2004; 2006).

Following are rules for the creation of chemistry in the negotiation process:

- **Shared interests**—Listen and begin at the point in which there is a common denominator. Really listening to what the other party is saying or not saying is absolutely vital for a successful negotiation. You must understand what the other side's needs are—this is an important basis for communication. Do not begin from the point in which you are or from the places to which you intend to go according to your interests.

- **Cultural differences**—It is better to speak about the differences than to blur them or hide them. Respect the differences. Acknowledgment of the difference prevents suspicions and facilitates the desire to overcome misunderstandings. Leverage the differences to creativity and be careful using them in arguments or for personal glorification.

- **Systemic thinking**—See the whole picture and all the details. See how the entire topic influences others: clients, workers, owners, and so on.

- **Focus**—Emphasize the few critical and high priority issues and invest primary effort in them.

- **Dualism**—Assess the interests of both parties as having equal worth. The interests of one party are not preferable to those of the other one.

The last point, which addresses the parties' differences and sometimes even conflicting interests requires further discussion. First, even if there are many overlapping interests, there will always be a number of differences. On the one hand, you cannot give up your interests. On the other hand, you must respect the interests of the other party and find creative solutions for both sides. Second, the emphasis must be on the transaction today as opposed to hypotheses and promises for the future. In many negotiations, the organization is represented by managers or agents who are not necessarily the organization's main owners. These representatives have personal interests and their own agendas. Note the differences, and sometimes even the contradictions, between these interests. Sometimes, this is expressed in the commitment of the representative who does not have the power to realize this commitment, which is not necessarily the organization's interest. Sometimes, the representative doesn't act for the organization's benefit.

The Action Plan

Negotiations need to be conducted as a planned process that enables the merger to act effectively to achieve the process's strategic objective. If the management sees the negotiations process as focusing on the financial and legal assessment of the opposite party, the negotiations and effort will revolve around contracts and numbers instead of emphasizing the process of the creation of a partnership that leads to shared success. This type of process, which emphasizes the technical evaluation and the takeover, is a sure prescription for failure. In addition, it is necessary to remember that most of the people who engage in this process—lawyers, accountants, investments bankers, and others—disappear immediately following the closing and do not have any responsibility in the implementation and success in the years after the agreement. Therefore, a shared action plan for the implementation of the M&A is requisite before the final agreement is signed.

Professional managers and others of different seniority levels are often not informed of and do not participate in the negotiation process due to reasons of confidentiality. However, among these people are the managers who will be responsible for and who will play a large part in the operational integration of the organizations. Because they have remained outside of the process, critical details for implementation might not be taken into consideration. Things that appear simple but are critical for the operational and organizational adjustment, such as information systems, human resources systems, and organizational cultural differences and others, can constitute significant obstacles in the process of integrating the organizations.

Preparing and writing a shared action plan is the true test of predicting the M&A success. The program and the process of its preparation enable critical goals to be achieved before and after the agreement. This should include the following:

- Examination of the synergy potential before the agreement is signed and the final price is determined

- Examination of the difficulty in the creation of cooperation and work of teams from the two organizations

- The determination of a realistic time schedule to be implemented

- The implementation costs

- The understanding of the organizational cultural differences

- Definition of the procedures, roles, organizational structure, and shared work processes after the agreement

- Reduction or elimination of the period of uncertainty—"the rumor factory"—which might lead to the departure of managers and key persons, and costs. The period of uncertainty, the tension, and the decline in output after the signing of the contract are characteristics of M&As and continue generally for many months and might cause the entire process to fail.

- The achievement of the commitment of the managers from both organizations that will be responsible for the implementation of the integration

The process of preparing the plan is as important as its content. The process enables the examination of the ability to solve problems together and to create a shared "language." It should be done before the agreement is signed so as not to create surprises following the agreement. The process enables the creation of chemistry, the construction of trust, the elimination of uncertainty, the vaporizing of rumors, the clarification of the future roles and responsibilities, and the achievement of organizational support for the idea of the M&A and its implementation.

Some devote to the process a 3-day seminar outside of the organization and examine the shared work under conditions that are at a certain stress level. Alternatively, you can construct a series of encounters, especially in the period of waiting for the approvals from the authorities, as long as there is no sweeping opposition to all contact on the part of the antitrust authority. In every process chosen, if the managers do not succeed in writing a detailed plan together, there is a low chance for successful shared management of the merger. As a senior manager at IBM said, "If you have finished all the answers before you have finished all the questions, then it is a sign that you haven't thought enough about the plan."

The main tenets of the process include the establishment of a steering team and the selection of people for this team, the selection of team heads, and the definition of the roles of the steering committee and the teams, the implementation of the teams according to a work plan, and schedules and reporting procures. All is undertaken according to worksheets, criteria, and tables, defined ahead of time, and planned processes of inspection and control.

The Process of Negotiations and Preparations

The true challenge in M&A negotiations does not lie in the differences of positions between the two management teams but in the conflicts that exist between the needs, desires, concerns, and interests of them. The negotiations are different from the case of the acquisition of real estate, a home, a car, furniture, or the procurement of equipment to create raw materials or service. Here, the formation requires a certain type of negotiation that enables the creation of synergy through shared work. In mergers, the objective of win-win in negotiations is to increase the "size of the cake" through the sharing of the creative and synergetic force of the parties instead of concern over who will receive the larger part of the cake at the expense of the other.

The struggle between the parties, in many cases, derives from the outlook that sees negotiations to be a situation of zero-sum game. The assumption at the basis of this perception is that there is a limited quantity of possibilities and resources and that what each party receives is always at the expense of the other party. Therefore, if the other party in the negotiations profits from something, necessarily this will be at the expense of the first party. In the negotiations, this perception has known meanings. From a position of a perception of power—even if it is erroneous—the requirements or suggestions will be extreme and not realistic. One of the known tactics is arguments of "we don't have the authority to decide"—after the discussion has reached a certain level and sensitive information has even been given: The negotiator thus shifts the decision to another party considered more senior. Another known tactic is the manipulation of emotions, when one side attempts to instill in the other party feelings of guilt, to emphasize special personal needs or to argue for special rights. These approaches, based on the zero-sum approach, prevent the synergetic cooperation that causes both sides to grow and profit. These approaches lead to a situation of win-lose, following which one side, which feels it has lost, or even worse, it has been cheated and will search for opportunities in the continuation to compensate itself at the expense of the profiting side. Hence, the cooperation is not real and is doomed to fail.

The alternative to zero-sum tactics is not a position of weakness. It is necessary to emphasize the advantages of your company and its strengths. There is nothing to fear in the bargaining for a good deal as long as it is fair. It is important to plan well for the negotiation process, and it can also help to use an outside consultant who is an expert both in the field and who has experience in M&A negotiations. Through such a consultant, sometimes during a 1-day or 2-day seminar, it is possible to work on all parts of the negotiations, such as opening, bargaining, and closing, and to prepare the negotiations strategy, objectives, opening positions, evaluations regarding the other party, and stages of progress (see Table 8.3).

Table 8.3   Conditions, Positions, and Objectives Toward and During the Negotiations

Key Topics	Opening Position	Compromise Position	Call-Off Position	Assessment of Other Side's Position	Possibilities for Giving Up and Returns for Achievement of Objectives
Topic 1					
Topic 2					
Topic 3					
Topic 4					
Topic 5					
Topic 6					

One of the goals of the first meetings in the negotiations is the collection of as much information as possible from the other party, its goals, modes of operation, organizational culture, management style, experience in previous M&As, future intentions, and so on. To obtain information, it is important to first define the essential information. Then, it is important to determine the list of appropriate questions. Lastly, it is important to decide upon the division of the areas of information and appropriate questions between the negotiations team people. All this, of course, will be determined in the framework of the preliminary planning. For the purposes of illustration, in the preparation for the negotiations conducted in the second half of 2002 between two companies in the food industry, the team of the divesting party determined approximately 80 questions in different areas of interest. (The company was acquired at 30 percent of its value assessment!) This type of preparation for negotiations broadcasts to the other party seriousness in the transaction and professionalism that contribute also to the power of negotiations and prevents tactics that are typical of the zero-sum approach. Moreover, preparations enable the determination of the red lines for the existence of the transaction, and this includes the deal's call-off price. Without precise preparation, such a price is not set, and the negotiations team might be dragged in the process to exaggerated prices. One of the leading hi-tech companies in Israel considered the acquisition of a suitable company for approximately 20 million dollars but got carried away and offered 160 million dollars for the same company. Last, it is necessary to analyze the bargaining power to correctly evaluate the interval for the negotiations during the process.

Following are examples of possible questions for the assessment of the sides' bargaining power:

- What are the alternatives that each party has?

- What is each party's degree of urgency to complete the transaction?

- To what extent is the other party interested in the M&A?

- What is the ratio between the resources that each party is supposed to invest?

- To what extent does the other party appreciate your strategic and operational advantages?

- To what extent is your involvement, in the post-agreement period, important to the other party?

Negotiations Team

The negotiations must be managed by a team instead of by one person. In all negotiations, there are advantages to a team versus single persons because a team can see and hear things that it is difficult for one person to assimilate. The team can have breathers to think, organize, digest, and take initiative in new directions that are frequently required in such a process. In addition, the team, as opposed to a single person, has important advantages in the framework of M&As. The team:

- Slows down the process and enables a thorough examination of the details, opportunities, and uncertainties.

- Enables a number of parallel conversations to be conducted in the negotiations. Thus, it saves time, enables in-depth entry into different areas, and enables additional channels of communication in case the negotiations get stuck.

- Enables a number of experts from different areas to be involved in the process.

- Enables intermediate managers, who will be responsible for the operational integration, to be involved and to have motivation for the implementation, and to present details that might be problematic in implementation.

- Enables the construction of teamwork with the other side toward a shared future.

Staffing the team requires considerable attention, and different areas and skills should be given the opportunity to be involved: people with negotiations abilities; people with knowledge in the financial field; a "crazy about it" leader; and a manager responsible for the integration. Effort should not be put forth to end the negotiations in a small number of meetings. Negotiations require time, and lack of patience weakens the bargaining power.

To conclude, it can be argued that despite all advice and recipes on M&A negotiation, it is still a complex and sensitive process. Each situation has a unique set of factors involving different forms of arrangements, different companies, people, territories, cultures, motives, and objectives. Therefore, above all, it is recommended that companies come to the negotiation table with a high degree of motivation, commitment, clarity, and trust.

References

Ahuja, G. and Katila, R. (2001). Technological acquisitions and the innovation performance of acquiring firms: a longitudinal study. *Strategic Management Journal*, 22: 197-220.

Angwin, D. (2001). Mergers and acquisitions across European borders: National perspectives on pre-acquisition due diligence and the use of professional advisors. *Journal of World Business*, 36 (1): 32-57.

Bleeke, J., and Ernst, D. (1993). *Collaborating to compete: Using strategic alliances and acquisitions in the global market place*. New York: John Wiley and Sons.

Child, J. and Faulkner, D. (1998). *Strategies of co-operation: Managing alliances, networks, and joint ventures*. New York: Oxford University Press.

Chung, S., Singh, H., and Lee, K. (2000). Complementarity, status similarity and social capital as drivers of alliance formation. *Strategic Management Journal*, 21, 1-22.

Donnelly, T., Morris, D., and Mellahi, K. (2002) The European automobile industry: Escape from parochialism. *European Business Review*, 14, 30-39.

Dyer, J., Kale, P., and Singh, H. (2004). When to ally & when to acquire. *Harvard Business Review*, 82 (7/8), 108-116.

Fisher, R., and Ury. W. (1981). In Child, J., and Faulkner, D. (1998). *Strategies of co-operation: Managing alliances, networks, and joint ventures*. New York: Oxford University Press.

Financial Times, 14th June 2000; Donnelly, T., Morris, D., and Mellahi, K. (2002) "European Automobile Industry: Escape from Parochialism." *European Business Review, 14: 30–39*.

Gomes, E. (2009). *Acquisitions in the UK car industry: A comprehensive analysis of the merger processes*. Saarbrucken: VDM Verlag Dr Muller AG & Co. KG.

Gomes, E., Cheema, P., and Janavaras, B. (2008). Effect of national cultural differences on the performance of cross-border mergers: Case of Indian companies going abroad. *Journal of International Business Research and Practice*, 1 (1): 79-96.

Goold, M., Campbell, A., and Alexander, M. (1994). *Corporate level strategy: Creating value in the multibusiness company*. New York: John Wiley & Sons.

Inkpen, A., Sundaram, A., and Rockwood, K. (2000). Cross-border acquisitions of U.S. Technology assets. *California Management Review, 42 (3), 50-71.*

Jemison, D. and Sitkin, S. (1986). The process can be a problem. *Harvard Business Review,* 107-116.

Kitching, J. (1967) op. cit. Barret, P. (1973). *The Human Implications of Mergers and Takeovers.* London: Institute of Personal Management; Schweiger, D. M., and Weber, Y. (1989). "Strategies for managing human resources during mergers and acquisitions: An empirical investigation." *Human Resource Planning,* 12: 69–86; Weber, Y., Shenkar, O., and Rave, A. (1996). "National and corporate culture fit in [mergers and acquisitions]: An exploratory study." *Management Science,* 42(8), 1215–27; Donnelly, T., Morris, D. and Mellahi, K. op. cit.

Kitching, J. (1967). "Why do mergers miscarry?" *Harvard Business Review,* November–December, 84–101; Leighton, C. and Tod, R. (1969). "After the acquisition: Continuing challenge." *Harvard Business Review,* March–April, 90–102; Donnelly, T., Morris, D., and Mellahi, K. (n.d.). "ROVER-BMW: Study in merger failure." *Coventry University, Business School,* Occasional Paper; Angwin, D. (2001). "Mergers and acquisitions across European borders: National perspectives on pre-acquisition due diligence and the use of professional advisors." *Journal of World Business,* 36(1), 32–57; Gomes, E., Cheema, P., and Janavaras, B. (2008). "Effect of national cultural differences on the performance of cross-border mergers: Case of Indian companies going abroad." *Journal of International Business Research and Practice,* 1 (1); Gomes, E. (2009). *Acquisitions in the UK Car Industry: A Comprehensive Analysis of the Merger Processes.* VDM Verlag Dr Muller Aktiengesellschaft & C0. KG: Saarbrucken. Gomes, E., Donnelly, T. Collis, C. and Morris, D. (Forthcoming, 2010). *Mergers and Acquisitions as Strategic Methods of Business Development in the Global Automobile Industry: An Analysis of Five Cases.* New York: The Edwin Mellen Press.

Pritchett, P., Robinson, D., and Clarkson, R. (1997). After the merger: *The authoritative guide for integration success.* Second Edition New York: McGraw-Hill.

Salacuse, Jeswald W. 1998. Research Report: Ten Ways that Culture Affects Negotiating Style: Some Survey Results. *Negotiation Journal,* July, 1998 (221).

Saorín, MC. (2004). Choices in joint ventures and acquisition negotiation behavior. *Management Research,* 2 (3), 219–234.

Saorin-Iborra, M. C. 2008. Time pressure in M&A negotiations: its determinants and effects on parties' negotiation behavior choice. *International Business Review,* 17, 285-309.

Schweiger, D., Csiszar, E., and Napier, N. (1993). "Implementing international mergers and acquisitions." *Human Resource Planning*, 16, 1: 53–70; Morosini, P. (1998). *Managing Cultural Differences*. Oxford: Pergamon Press; Testa, G. and Morosini, P. (2001). "How to win in execution: the Role of leadership in CNH Construction Equipment M&As and Alliances." In: *Berlin Carnegie Bosch Institute Conference on Internacional Management*. October.

9

EXTENDED DUE DILIGENCE EXAMINATION AND SUMMATIVE EVALUATION FOR M&AS

After the decision has been made, by both parties, and a memorandum of understanding (MOU) or letter of intention (LOI) have been sent, it is necessary to perform a due diligence. This process constitutes an examination of all the topics related to acquisition to ensure that the acquiring company has (or both parties in the merger have) all the relevant information of the acquired company before the deal is finished and paid for. This chapter extends the accepted perception regarding the scope of the due diligence. In addition to the normal examinations in such fields as the finance and legal issues, this chapter recommends the performance of a comprehensive examination of the two primary factors that determine the success of most M&As: the potential for synergy and the ability to realize this potential as expressed, mainly, in the differences in the management/organizational culture between the parties in the transaction.

The Process and Goals of Due Diligence

The process of due diligence is a multistage process that includes a review of the legal, financial, strategic, managerial, and other aspects of documents, contractors, organizational structures, and the entire operations of the acquired party. In essence, due diligence is the examination of the reality versus all the factors that motivated the deal and caused it to appear interesting: Does reality correspond with the vision? Issues of confidentiality cause the information that reaches the acquiring party to be limited in the initial stages of the negotiations, and issues of marketing cause the divesting party or its representative to emphasize the advantages of the business to be sold and not to focus on its disadvantages. The process of due diligence can also find additional positive aspects, but experience shows that generally it is the acquired party's and the deal's shortcomings that are found. The acquirer has a number of options: i) to purchase the company according to the contract if the disadvantages are not significant, ii) to negotiate the transaction price, or iii) to abandon the deal.

Due diligence generally is performed by a number of teams, where the size of these teams is determined by the complexity of the transaction:

- **Financial/accounting**—Performed by accounting and financial personnel
- **Legal**—Performed by lawyers or legal departments
- **Business strategy**—Performed by the company management and its consultants

During the process, it is important that the teams exchange information about the risks and potential problems of the acquired party's operations and of the attempt to realize synergies. The process, when performed appropriately, can be exhausting, require a long period of time, be disappointing, and is expensive. However, it is essential for the merger success, and the process is supposed to provide important information on the target company and the costs and risks of the acquisition. The acquirer needs to expect that the target will be defensive, resisting, and impatient in the due diligence process. Most managers do not enjoy having their decisions/activities precisely examined, especially if the process takes a long time and leads to uncertainty about their future.

An effective due diligence process requires considerable professionalism because it influences the future of relations between the parties and in worst cases can result in the end of the deal. In the process, considerable skill is required in the choice of the correct questions, the manner of asking the questions, the choice of the people to answer the questions, and even the timing of the questions. The process requires the ability to create an atmosphere that includes trust, but also fear, so that reliable and complete information is conveyed. The key point is to identify the special problems of the target—a standard list of questions will not be adequate for all businesses.

The process consists of multiple stages. First, in the basic data collection process, the main topics will be identified. Then, there will be questions that arise from the data analysis and will require further data collection according to the special problems of the M&A. The stages will repeat themselves as necessary. However, it is necessary to remember that this is a difficult process and therefore caution and great consideration are required so as not to cut off the entire merger deal.

Extension of the Due Diligence Examination

It is surprising to see how little attention such factors as differences in culture and human capital receive in the decision-making processes of managements that consider M&As. This especially since today it is a well-known fact that the percentages of success of mergers is low, and differences in management/organizational culture are the decisive factor in the success of the M&A. In practice, managements rarely discuss and decide whether to acquire a company according to the risk in the implementation of the M&A that derives from cultural differences. Generally, the management is satisfied with the data that arise from the traditional due diligence examination that addresses the financial/accounting and legal aspects. It is likely that this situation derives from the fact that the managers and consultants do not know how to methodically measure the level of cultural differences and therefore find it difficult to discuss a topic that is vague to the point of virtuality. This book presents and describes the methods and management instruments through which it is possible to perform a good measurement of cultural differences and to enable the management

- To reach the correct decision whether the discussed M&A is suitable for the organization

- To know what is the correct price that can be paid for the deal, taking into account the differences in culture and possible difficulties of implementation

- To plan the stages of integration while dealing with challenges of cultural differences and retaining the human capital

- To set targets of negotiations relevant to the implementation challenges

Thus, this book extends the traditional due diligence examination and includes also the examination of differences in management culture and human capital of the acquired/merged company and the methodical evaluation of the existing synergy potential.

Topics for the Examination of Due Diligence

Research published in 2001 found that managers ascribe differing importance to the topics of due diligence according to their country of origin. For example, the Germans and Swiss think that due diligence is important for the understanding of the industry to which they enter, whereas in contrast, the Swedes, the Dutch, the French, and the English think that due diligence examination is important for the understanding of other issues. The Dutch, for example, attribute great importance in the evaluation of cultural differences and in the planning of the integration process, whereas the Germans think this is less important.

In the following sections, different topics of due diligence are described without referring to their order of importance and with only examples being provided. In reality, it is necessary to adjust the questions to every M&A, and as aforementioned, some of the special questions will be raised in coming stages after the collection and analysis of initial information.

Legal Topics

The team of the acquirer and the legal consultants will, in the due diligence process, collect data so that they can answer a great number of legal questions. The process will allow them to know what are the legal steps to be adopted to succeed in the deal, such as the agreement of shareholders, directors, banks, venture funds, government/authorities (such as the Anti-Trust Authority, the courts, and the bank supervisor) and even the main customers. The team will examine whether the acquirer can expect legal problems for assuming the divesting party's obligations to different factors, short term and long term. Examples include obligations to inter-organizational parties such as government authorities that enforce issues of environmental pollution, taxation, and so on or internal factors such as workers' claims for compensation. The following list of legal topics makes no aspiration to be complete but indicates a variety of examples for legal examination:

I. Topics of Incorporation, Regulation Code, and Shareholders

- Regulations and incorporation documents
- Protocols of directorate and shareholders' meetings
- Lists of shareholders, annual reports, and so on
- List of all the countries where the target is allowed to operate and the legal implications
- All the contracts and agreements between the target's shareholders

II. Financial Topics

- Loans and credit agreements with the shareholders
- Personal guarantees given by the shareholders or other parties for the target's debts
- Financial reports to the management council in the past 5 years
- All the correspondence with the taxation and other authorities
- Agreements with senior managers and key personnel regarding special payments, compensation in certain situations, and so on
- Issues related to multinational activity such as legal restrictions on activities, patent protection, export/import licenses, government supervision, and tariffs

III. Topics of Management and Worker Employment

- All worker employment contracts
- Agreements related to consultation, management, financial services, and professional attachment with external parties

- Collective agreements and agreements with unions or professional associations
- Safety and health files, including worker claims for compensation
- All the benefit programs for the workers, including
  - Pension and retirement
  - Profit distribution
  - Options and stocks
  - Insurances, including insurance for managers and directors, health insurance, and so on
- All the directives, procedures, and policies in the areas of human resources, such as recruitment, promotion, sexual harassment, vacations/holidays, reimbursement for expenses
- Personal information (addresses, phone numbers, and personal files) of every manager and key personnel that left the target during the past 3 years

IV. Tangible and Intangible Assets of the Target

- List of all the obligations for rent and leasing of assets, including place, address, renewal rights, and costs
- List of all real estate properties owned by the target, place, address, and characteristics, including obligations and risk, such as pollution
- List of all other tangible assets
- Mortgages, taxes, insurances, and all the agreements related to the target's assets
- List of all the patents, patents in process, trademarks, rights, Internet addresses, licenses, licensing, and all agreements and correspondence related to intellectual capital
- Copies of all the researches, evaluations, opinions, and other reports related to the target's assets

V. Contracts and Other Obligations

- All the sales and procurement contracts of products, materials, equipment, devices, services, and so on
- Documents that indicate expansion programs in the target's facilities
- Research contracts
- Distribution contracts, licenses, licensing, and agencies

- Alliance and strategic collaboration agreements and joint initiatives
- Agreements that limit the target's rights to compete in any area
- Contracts on the purchase, sale, removal of electricity, gas, water, telephone, waste, or any other service
- List of all the materials related to environmental pollution and treatment of these materials, including removal and storage sites
- Agreements with logistic firms, shippers, and delivery services
- Credit letters
- Licenses, permits, and governmental certification for the target that are required to operate the business and that, when the ownership is changed, might expire or not be renewed

VI. Claims

- List of all claims or arguments related to quality of the product or service sold to customers, claims on the part of the workers, government actions, and other cautions
- Opinion of the lawyer suing in the name of or defending the target for every claim
- List of all compromise agreements, mediations, and so on
- Description of the labor relations systems, strikes, and so on
- All the correspondence with governmental authorities

VII. Other

- The curriculum vitae of all the senior management members and key personnel
- Different announcements to the press in the past 3 years
- Market researches, surveys, and expert reports in the industry
- List of all the consultants and experts employed by the target in the past 3 years
- Standard forms found in use, such as procurement forms and sales forms

Business and Operational Topics

In parallel to the legal team, another team engages in due diligence on the business and operational topics. In this process, the team might discover a series of problems and need to evaluate the risk they entail and the profitability of the deal. Typical such problems are unhealthy dependence on a low number of customers or suppliers, incorrect valuations of inventory or unsellable stock, bad debts that are not recorded as such, tax debts, inappropriate information systems, immediately required investment because of outdated equipment, inventory, computerization systems, and so on.

The acquirer interested in a company operating in a different, unfamiliar industry will have additional important questions to address: What are the key factors of success in the industry? What is the image and reputation of the target's business in this sector? Does the target operate in a certain segment? Is the market share increasing or decreasing? Why? What are the steps required to improve the target's business situation? What are the costs for doing so? The following list of topics is again not exhaustive and includes a variety of examples:

I. Money

- Analysis of all the financial reports: examination of the financial relations, cash flow, trends of recent years compared to the industry and foremost competitors; examination according to products, geographic regions, channels of distribution, and so on.

- Does the deal influence the financial data (including the earnings per share of the acquiring company)?

- What are the billing practices and debt collection practices? What is the average credit to customers? Are there any bad debts from previous years? How does the system for collecting debts operate and how reliable is it?

- What is the capital structure of the company? What are the leverage relations? What are the short-term and long-term debts?

- Financial forecasts for the coming years according to products, geographic regions, and so on. What are the main sources of growth and profitability for the coming years? What are the expected results? Predictions of threats and risks in different areas, including international activities?

II. Operations

- How does the target's logistics system operate? Transport costs? Supervision of raw materials? What are the inventory levels?

- What are the methods of production? What is the level of efficiency? Capacity and exploitation of capacity? Ability to expand and the costs this entails? Level of flaws? Dependence on seasonality and cycles?

- How do the equipment, the plant, and the different facilities operate? What are the level and cost of maintenance? When will equipment, machinery, facilities, and devices need to be replaced and what will be the cost?

- Does the target operate according to production plans, schedules, and reports? How is the data obtained? Is there room for progress in the experience curve? Is there commitment and are there agreements to acquire raw materials? What is the procurement policy?

- What are the operations policy and procedures?

III. Marketing and Sales

- What are the target's groups of customers and markets? What are the main products/services? Addresses, telephones, and names of main customers, their size, their financial situation, forecasts of their demand, and the average length and size of customer relationships? How much efforts are placed on customer acquisition versus customer retention?

- What are the market shares of each area of engagement?

- What are the threats and opportunities in each one of the areas of engagement? What are the trends, and what are the forecasts for all the relevant factors of the environment such as economic, legal, governmental/political, social/cultural/ demographic, and technological environments? Customers, suppliers, competitors, job market, and so on? An analysis of the forces in the industry, including degree of rivalry, entry barriers, substitutes, and so on is required.

- What are the methods of distribution? Comparison to those of competitors in the field.

- Description and analysis of competitors, their strengths, and their weaknesses. What are their development and strategic trends? Analysis of their financial reports, reputation, variety of products and services, and level of differentiation and its elements for each of their products.

- The same information regarding, and detailed characteristics of, the customers.

- What is the target's marketing strategy? What are its plans in the areas of advertisement and publicity, promotion of sales, public relations, and so on? What is the degree of effectiveness of the plans?

- How are the target's processes of data collection, business intelligence gathering, and marketing research implemented?

IV. The Management and How It Manages

The topic of organizational culture is discussed separately:

- What is the organizational structure and how is it reflected in the organization chart? What are the role descriptions? How up to date are they? How are authorities and responsibilities delegated? What are the communication methods in the organization?

- What are the work relations in the organization? What is the history of strikes?

- What are the background, experience, and education of the senior managers and key personnel?

- What are the methods of recruitment, promotion, instruction, performance evaluation, and reward in the organization?

- What is the level of turnover in the organization in the management and among the workers? In recent years, did key personnel leave? How many and from what positions?

- What is the strategy of the target? What is the process of strategy preparation? What is the process of choice of strategy? How is the information used, and what is the level of description and analysis? What is the degree of use of business intelligence? Was there planning for the process of the strategy implementation? Were measurable objectives set? Were analytical instruments used?

- What are the methods of supervision/inspection in the organization?

- What is the mission/vision of the organization? Is the vision/mission phrased formally?

- Description of the information systems in the organization, their management, their effectiveness, and maintenance and exchange requirements.

V. Research and Development (R&D)

- Description of R&D strategies, key personnel, and primary activities.

- Situation of the new products, estimated time to market, required development costs, required technologies, and risks.

- Patents and patents in process.

- R&D relations with other factors, alliances, strategies, and joint initiatives.

Due Diligence Examination of Organizational Culture

Differences in management/organizational culture can impair the integration process, the ability to realize the synergy potential, and can even cause the failure of the entire merger. There are several examples of this, such as the mergers of ECI and Tadiran, Creo and Scitex, and Madge and Linnet. Therefore, evaluation and measurement of the differences of organizational/management culture are required so that the decision makers of both sides of the merger can decide whether they are interested in the merger. If the answer is affirmative, then they must properly prepare for the expected difficulties, set the correct price for the acquisition, plan the process of integration of companies and know to retain key personnel, who, in most mergers, leave especially when there are great cultural differences.

A comprehensive due diligence of culture—if the time and resources allow it—will include six stages: i) planning, ii) research, iii) decision on methods of evaluation and measurement, iv) measurement and collection of data, v) summary, report, and recommendations, and vi) the integration process and its implementation. In the following sections, short descriptions of the six stages are provided.

I. Planning

It is necessary to define and identify areas, topics, and divisions for which the evaluation of cultures will be undertaken as well as the required degree of confidentiality. It is further necessary to clarify the level of access regarding every organization, division, and the people to be contacted for evaluation and measurement. It is necessary to define the requirements of data collection, the materials, the documents, and the reports in the process. For example, in stage 2, it is necessary to coordinate and obtain permission regarding the schedule, roles, responsibility, and logistics entailed by the process: What will be the formal documents to learn from regarding the management culture? Who will be interviewed and when? How will measurement devices, including questionnaires on culture, be used?

II. Research

The collection and analysis of data, such as the CEO statement, the written vision/ mission statement, internal communication, annual reports, material for new workers, organization charts, material on the company website, publications for customers, and so on. Additional collected material includes worker surveys on morale, work climate, and so on. In addition, information on "soft" processes, such as reward characteristics for different behaviors, leaders, and how they shape behavior, is collected. What are the means of communication and how is information transferred?

III. Decision on Methods of Evaluation and Measurement

From the analysis of the material in the research process, key topics surface and decisions are made regarding the methods and scope of data collection—interviews, focus groups, use of questionnaires—on the basis of accessibility and required confidentiality. The stages and schedule for the data collection and analysis and the sample size are decided.

IV. Measurement and Collection of Data

Interviews with key personnel and managers on the senior management level, distribution of questionnaires, interviews with key personnel on operational levels and in selected units from the two organizations. Interviews with negotiation team members and due diligence teams.

V. Summary, Report, and Recommendations

Preparation of a report and presentation for the senior management of the acquirer or both firms and for the steering committee of the integration process. The report will include analysis of the general cultural differences, in the different divisions, and the different dimensions of the culture. Evaluations should be noted regarding the degree of influences and failures expected from the cultural differences in the different areas of integration. A way of coping with the challenges of implementation in the different stages of the integration of the organizations and with the influences on the human dimension and the prevention of the departure of managers and key personnel should be recommended. This should be linked to possibilities of the realization of the synergy potential and with the decision to choose the appropriate integration approach for the discussed M&A.

VI. The Integration Process and Its Implementation

The findings should be presented to the managers in the launch meeting of the integration process and to the members of the teams in the following integration stages. It is necessary to focus the team members on the verification of the data, the ways of coping with the implementation challenges, process of supervision/inspection of the changes of culture recommended, and the effects expected in the integration process.

Evaluations Regarding Synergy Potential and Realization

This part extends the accepted due diligence examinations by adding the analysis of the potential of synergy in the merger and the possibility to implement this synergy, taking into consideration organizational cultural differences, expected costs, and required schedules. A thorough due diligence provides a more in-depth understanding to the teams about the target company's resources, management skills, and its competitive advantages and disadvantages. Now the acquiring company can analyze the synergy potential in a more in-depth manner from the analysis undertaken on the cultural differences.

The information accumulated enables the more precise identification of sources of the creation of value, such as the unification of functions and increased efficiency, distribution channels, assistance of complementary products, transfer of professional knowledge in different areas, and so on. Tables 9.1 and 9.2 outline these areas, and they are also summarized here:

- Sources and areas of synergy
- Manner of exploitation of the synergy (in which organization the functions and/ or activities will be united, to whom the knowledge will be transferred, and so on)
- Evaluation of the time required to implement every source of synergy
- Financial evaluation of the advantages that derive from the exploitation of the synergy in each area and according to the planned schedule
- Requirements and conditions for the implementation in the integration process
- Costs required in the integration process that will lead to the exploitation of synergy

Table 9.1   Synergy in the Field of _____

Number	Description for Realization and Implementation of Synergy Potential	Financial Value (000)	Schedule	Relationship to Task Force / Other Area

Table 9.2   Example of Costs in the Integration Process

Field and Topics	Cost	Responsibility	Basis for Evaluation
Move Offices			
Renovate/build rooms			
New furniture			
Telephones/computers			
Information Systems			
Suitability of information systems			
Acquisition of software			

Field and Topics	Cost	Responsibility	Basis for Evaluation
Marketing Sales Changes in packaging Advertisement in the press Announcement to clients			
Human Resources Termination compensation Worker placement Workshops, dealing with organizational cultural differences			
Monies Suitability of reporting systems Suitability of money collection system			
Production/Operations Changes in production processes Transfer of production lines			
Legal Expenses Copyright/trademark/patents Legal counsel in negotiations and work union agreements			

In addition, you must describe strategic advantages from the merger process such as strategic options and opportunities following the M&A. Such opportunities can be help for other businesses in the corporation; access to further market segments; ability to achieve financing for R&D and other investments; tax advantages; reputation; ability to forge alliances; the creation of new strategies, and so on.

In summary, the process of extended examination of due diligence requires the considerable planning, cooperation, and patience of the acquirer and the target. Every attempt to shorten the process will cause mishaps in the future, lengthen the implementation process, and can bring about failure of the merger. Attempts to give false presentations or conceal data will bring about legal claims after the contract is signed. The evaluations should be summarized in a special report to be submitted to the acquiring company's management. Without such description, there is great fear that the acquirer will enter a merger in which it should not have been involved or alternatively will avoid a merger that actually would have been greatly beneficial.

Do's and Do Not's

- Do: It is necessary to plan all the stages of the extended due diligence and to include the required information, the way in which the information was achieved, who will do what in the different teams, the schedule, and so on.

- Do: The examination process will dedicate an extended place to measure analysis of the differences in organizational culture and the expected implications on the implementation of the merger and the integration process.

- Do: The process will describe at length the analysis of the synergy potential and will include financial evaluations of the synergy in the different fields, the required schedule for implementation, costs and means required for the exploitation of the synergy, strategic advantages, and so on.

- Do: It is necessary to ascertain that the team from the acquirer is suited for the examination of the acquired company's documents, for example, the examination of complicated financial reports, complicated technical reports, and so on.

- Do: It is necessary to ascertain that the team of the acquirer is suited for the examination of due diligence and is welcomed by the target, receives cooperation, and can maintain a good, open, and clear communication that prevents misunderstandings and mishaps—this process is important for the target as well as for the acquirer.

- Do Not: It is important that the divesting party does not conceal data or beautify it; otherwise, it might enter an undesired merger and even be sued after the agreement for falsification.

10
AGREEMENTS

The negotiation process enters into an important stage after preliminary meetings have taken place, seller and buyer understand each other's perspectives and objectives, and in an ideal case, the process of screening elicits the preferred candidate for both sides. The next step is the preparation of a precontractural written agreement that defines the respective preliminary understanding and conducts a process in which both parties agree to get to know each other better toward a long-term relationship. This process must be clear, well organized, and carefully orchestrated to make sure the definitive agreement fits the goals of both parties, serves as a roadmap for upcoming steps, and lays the ground for successful implementation of the merger. To this end, a Letter of Intent (LOI) or Memorandum of Understanding (MOU) serves such process and the process of due diligence described in Chapter 9, "Extended Due Diligence Examination and Summative Evaluation for M&As."

Letter of Intention (LOI) or Memorandum of Understanding (MOU)

An essential change in the manner of the negotiations occurs. Here the understandings and conversations made during preliminary meetings are transformed to the stage of writing and phrasing, which clarifies the existing agreements and lack of agreements. There are arguments against written documents, which may have obligating legal meaning. However, most of the executives involved in negotiations feel more comfortable when the intentions of each side and the business framework are defined in an LOI before more time and money are invested in the process. In most cases, the LOI is not intended to be binding except under very special conditions and circumstances. Furthermore, with the LOI, both sides make a psychological commitment to the merger and to more formal negotiations.

There are different styles of the LOI, which change according to the business's legal counsel. Generally, these documents have items that are: (1) binding, (2) not binding, or (3) mixed. The choice of the style is made according to the following considerations:

- The costs to both acquirer and target firm entailed by the continuation of the process before the commitment is made

- The assessment of the parties of the date at which it is possible to reach the definitive agreement

- The necessity to reveal various type of information to the public, primarily in publicly traded companies

- The presence (or absence) of additional candidates for the proposed merger

In most cases, a mixed document, which contains both binding and nonbinding sections, is the most effective. The document includes important principles and constitutes the initial starting point for the final agreement. A letter of intent generally creates a psychological commitment and leads to seriousness and depth in the negotiations because it also defines the areas that require clarifications and that still require final agreement.

Typical sections in the LOI are

- **Valuation of the transaction**—The price to be paid in cash or shares, in trust and/or in payments that can depend on the future performances and other predetermined conditions. This can be expressed as a mechanism (for example, five times the Annual Revenue or EBITDA) as opposed to a set figure.

- **Structure of the transaction**—Description of the nature of the M&A, such as assets, equipment, activity, obligations, and the mode of payment, cash and/or in shares.

- **The governance and mode of management**—The size of the board of directors, the head of the board, voting rights, and voting percentage required to make decisions in principle. When the CEO/owners of the acquired company remain in the organization, and especially in the case of the acquisition of 50 percent or less of the company shares, the divesting party will be required to define the independence in decisions and rights for the continuation of the business operation. This is a sensitive and an important issue, both for the remaining management and for the acquirer, who is interested that this management will continue to operate the business at a high level of commitment after the agreement as well. Here is the place to define many topics such as the appointment of senior managers, the level of investments, the goals and strategies without the need for the board of directors' approval, the setting of the salary and bonuses, and the many other issues that are important to the management and to the operation of the business, which until now were undertaken independently.

- **Closing**—The closing date and documents required to close the deal.

- **Due diligence**—This defines stages, schedules, and access to the company's documents. It also describes the disclosure of data, such as financial and operational reports, contracts and agreements, plans, assets, managers and employees by the executives, stockholders, consultants, and other representatives of the acquiring company.

- **No shop**—The seller obligates itself not to conduct negotiations with other firms on the topic of M&As as long as the buying company conducts the examinations required to close the M&A and sign the binding document. In most cases, this period is restricted in time to 2 to 3 months.

- **Confidentiality**—The buyer and its managers obligate themselves to maintain full confidentiality in respect to the data that were exposed to them including their conclusions.

- **Expenses**—The M&A process involves costs, such as fees for various consultants and firms. Therefore, the LOI defines which party carries these expenses. In addition, the buying company is interested in defining compensations in case the seller decides not to continue with the deal. Similarly, the seller wants compensation in case the buyer withdraws from the transaction or cannot fulfill it, for instance, as the consequence of failure to finance the deal.

- **Management contracts and employees' agreements**—The LOI describes important conditions about buyer managers and employees including, for instance, the amounts of compensation if some are fired or leave of their own free will.

- **Conditions for definitive agreement**—Both parties want to define the key terms or circumstances under which they will not be obligated to the transaction, such as a sharp drop in the stock values, lost of main customers, and so on.

- **Conduct of the business until the deal closing**—The buyer usually wants some protection that from the signing of the LOI until the closing of the deal there are no essential changes in the acquired business that might be detrimental to its value. For example, the operation of the business is expected to continue as before without the sale of important assets and/or the increase of business commitments. In addition, the seller is expected to keep good maintenance of equipment and correct handling of customers, etc.

To conclude, an LOI is an engagement process in which both sides agree to attempt to get to know each other as they prepare to embark on a long-term relationship. This process needs to be organized appropriately. Table 10.1 describes a suggested schedule and duties for such a synchronized process. Yet, the process might last a longer period of time. For instance, the due diligence in large M&As requires more time than average M&As, primarily if the seller has a large number of different locations and activities in a number of countries. In addition, the process of the approval from authorities, such as anti-trust agencies and from the board of directors, might take a long time. Therefore, the time schedule should be defined by both parties so any delay will be expected and, thus, avoid disappointments and lack of trust that might lead to an end of the process before the deal actually takes place.

Table 10.1   Proposal for a Schedule and Tasks from the Signing of the Letter of Intent to the Closing*

Time	Task	Responsibility
7-8 weeks before closing	1. Signing the LOI, approval of the managers/board of director councils of the negotiations.	Both parties & consultants
	2. Due diligence requirements conveyed to divesting party	Acquirer
6-7 weeks before closing	1. Organization of material for due diligence and sending it to the acquirer	Divesting party
	2. Examination of due diligence	Acquirer's teams & consultants
	3. Preparation of drafts for contracts	Lawyers of both parties
	4. Comprehensive examination of target's financial reports	Acquirer's accountant
5-6 weeks before closing	1. Negotiations examinations & corrected drafts of contract	Consultants of both parties
	2. Approvals of directors & shareholders	Managements of the parties
	3. Preparation of documents for third party for confirmation (supervisor of insurance or banks, primary clients, anti-trust authorities, etc.)	Consultants of the parties
	4. Preparation of summative report on examinations & submission to CEO	Acquirer's team

3 weeks before closing	1. Reciprocal examination of material for press & media & other factors	Management teams of the parties
	2. Scheduling to close all the required documents	Management teams of the parties
1-2 weeks before closing	1. All details of the negotiations of the last moment	Consultants of the parties
	2. Receipt of required approvals, for instance, tax payments	Consultants of the parties
	3. Examination of other approvals such as the board of directors' decisions	Consultants of the parties

*Adopted from *Mergers and Acquisition Management* (Weber, 2003).

The Acquisition Agreement

When the due diligence, valuations, and appraisals have been completed, and terms and price are agreed, the acquisition team must work carefully to prepare the acquisition agreement. Unlike a typical LOI, this agreement is a legally binding agreement. A party that fails to consummate the transaction without a legal excuse can be liable for damages.

Usually, the initial draft of the agreement is typically prepared by the buyer's counsel, The buyer wants to assure that the acquired assets and liabilities are purchased without assuming responsibilities for any undisclosed obligations of the business or the seller. The negotiation of the acquisition agreement is mainly an allocation of the risks to each party both before and after closing. In other words, a key aspect of the negotiation is the allocation of the risk of economic loss attributable to legal and some financial defects in the target company that might surface after the closing.

The buyer is usually concerned with risks associated with misrepresentation or breach of covenant by the seller and by circumstances that were not necessarily anticipated at the time of the negotiation. For example, a lawsuit against the target company might come after the acquisition takes place such as because the plant site of the seller is found to be a toxic waste dump due to negligence of the seller management. Thus, the acquiring company will often seek a full indemnity from the acquired company against any liabilities that have not been assumed by the acquiring company as part of the transaction and any damages or losses that were incurred due to the inaccuracy of the representations, warranties, or agreements.

Thus, the agreement accomplishes several goals:

a. It articulates the structure and terms of the deal.

b. It describes the important legal and financial aspects of the seller company.

c. It binds buyer and seller to their best in order to complete the transaction.

d. It binds the seller to keep the acquired company in good condition without major changes before the deal is closed.

e. It guides the parties how to act in case of new problems that have been disclosed before the closing but were not properly disclosed.

To accomplish these goals, a typical agreement will have the following sections:

a. The price and mechanisms of the transaction

b. Representations and warranties of the seller and buyer

c. Conditions precedent to closing

d. Conduct of business prior to closing

e. Indemnification

f. Termination procedures and remedies

Item a refers also to the structure of the transaction such as stock disposition or asset disposition. In an asset acquisition, it identifies which assets are to be conveyed to the buying company. In a case of a merger, the consideration per share to be received by exchanging shareholders will be described as well as other important issues such as the composition of its board of directors and names of its top executives and their positions.

Item b usually sets forth the financial responsibilities of the buyer and seller if certain unknown or unforeseen problems arise after closing the deal owing to an existing situation. From the buyer's point of view, post-closing events that reduce revenues and assets or increase liabilities due to undisclosed issues are the responsibility of the seller. Thus, the seller has to make detailed statements on a wide range of written and binding representations and warranties to the buyer. These provisions will include legal and financial conditions of the acquired company and that the transaction is not in breach of any agreements and obligations of the company being sold, and all material facts including exhibits and schedules have been disclosed. This is very important because each party will be able to back out of the acquisition agreement if it discovers that the representations and warranties of the other party are untrue.

The section about conditions preceding the closing phase contains items that appear in Table 10.1 These steps and conditions have to be carefully considered because a failure to satisfy some of them might give the other party the right to walk away from the deal.

The seller has the obligation to keep the goodwill of the business and the condition of the assets during the time until closing the deal. The parties should also include in the negotiation the penalties for noncompliance such as reduced purchase price or even ability to walk away from the deal.

The indemnification section set forth the circumstances that each party can take remedial actions or claim damages in case the other party has failed to abide by its covenants.

The last section of the agreement describes the situations under which the deal can be terminated by each party and the consequences of termination. For example, it includes a date by which the closing must occur and the right to sue the party that breaches the contract.

Other agreements may take place such as a noncompetition agreement, Earn-Out agreement, and inter-creditor agreement among multiple lenders to a particular borrower.

How to Be Helped by Lawyers[1]

It is the management's, not the lawyers', role to lead the negotiations. Lawyers are supposed to provide counsel. Some recommend that lawyers are involved only in the closing stages of the process and the reasons for this position are convincing. Lawyers are supposed to protect their clients against future problems and unexpected situations. As aforementioned, the first stages are important to the creation of chemistry/trust and to the construction of the shared business basis that indicates the transaction's advantages to both parties. A lawyer can facilitate the formation of the trust and the emphasis of the benefits if he, as per the nature of his work, indicates the difficulties and problems. This happens when sufficient planning is absent in the early stages. The lawyer fills what is missing with ideas to prevent risks.

A draft of the contract in an early phase will foster fears in the other party, which will become resistant and painstaking in regards to the different technical details. However, merger transactions do not fail because of the contract's legal quality. It is preferable to focus on trust and agreements between parties instead of fears, and to enable the parties to be creative in making a worthwhile transaction. When the two parties decide that the transaction is worthwhile and even engage in the small details of the transaction, the lawyers can build the agreement according to both parties' viewpoints and wishes.

Some lawyers recommend a "departure strategy" from the transaction. They emphasize that a merger transaction should not be entered without beforehand solving the problem of separation/departure in case it does not succeed. This approach, however, sows the

---

1. Adopted from *Mergers and Acquisition Management* (Weber, 2003).

seeds of the separation of the transaction. The emphasis on the mode of departure distracts the attention from the strategic and operational opportunities and creates a focus on problems and threats rather than the opportunities.

While in the first stage, it is desirable not to bring the lawyers to the discussions; it is possible to seek their counsel on different important issues and it is certainly possible to involve them in the stages of the confidentiality agreements. If an LOI includes many items, similar to the final agreement, then of course it is necessary to involve the lawyer and definitely a process of due diligence cannot be undertaken without their thorough work.

It's preferable to choose a lawyer with experience in the field of M&As. Lawyers who have diplomatic abilities are preferable to those who sally forth into combat in negotiations. In addition, lawyers with knowledge in the field of taxation can be of tremendous help in determining the transaction structure and can bring about savings in costs.

There are several possibilities to save lawyer fees:

- Keep the lawyers "ring-side" (like a coach in a boxing match), so that they are involved and provide counsel from time to time but are not complete partners in the initial stages of the negotiations.

- In the situation of a small organization versus a large organization, the large organization should be allowed to prepare the draft of the legal documents. Large organizations have lawyers on staff or as regular consultants and they have agreements in regular formats. The people of the large organization will feel confident and in control and the small organization will avoid these legal expenses in the first stages.

- A detailed and clear draft of the principles of the agreement should be developed as a basis for the legal documents. Otherwise, the lawyer will need to think about the possible risks, even if they are not relevant, and will prepare a long document to deal with possible uncertainties. Many such preparations will cost a lot of money and will lead to fears and rejection in the other party.

- Determine ahead of time a quota of hours or overhead cost for a project and set conditions for payment, related to the degree of progress and end of the contract.

PART IV

Post-Merger Integration and Implementation

11

MANAGEMENT OF CULTURE CLASH

A recent survey conducted by Boston Consulting Group (BCG) reveals that the top obstacle to successful integration of two companies in M&A is cultural differences between the acquirer and the target companies. This item was cited by 83 percent of the executives that were part of this survey. Indeed, the graveyard of business is full of M&As that have foundered, in whole or in part, on the shoals of culture and integration, such as Daimler-Benz and Chrysler, AOL and Time Warner, AT&T, and NCR. Yet, culture clash can be successfully managed!

Based on the details from Chapter 6, "Culture and Cultural Differences Analysis," you can estimate the level of cultural differences along various dimensions and at various areas. If an acquirer decides to buy the target firm in spite of cultural differences, for instance, because of a high level of synergy, the management will need to manage the culture clash between the two top management teams and employees. Left unattended, the culture clash will cause bitter conflicts, and sometimes intended sabotage, that will be detrimental to the implementation of the merger.

Many acquisitions with high potential for success failed because the buying company did not manage the conflicts caused by cultural differences. This management challenge is the subject of this chapter.

Culture Clash Evolution and Stages

Scholars of organizational conflict regard conflict as a process that includes antecedent conditions, affective states (for example, tension and stress), negative attitudes on the part of one group toward the other, and conflictual behavior that ranges from passive resistance to overt aggression. The first section here discusses cultural differences as the antecedent of these affective states and negative attitudes.

Prior to a merger or an acquisition, each firm's top management team (TMT) usually achieves some degree of equilibrium in understanding its external and internal environment, Over time and with shared experience among members, the people of each company assimilate beliefs and values that greatly influence its decision-making processes, behavior, procedures, reward system, and every aspect of organizational life. In the M&A, when one culture is exposed to another, as happens in the process of acculturation, the state of equilibrium is disturbed, which can lead to communication problems between the cultures. The shared beliefs and values, which are unique to each firm's culture and which originally functioned to facilitate communication among a team's members in each organization, become sources of communication problems between members of the two parties.

These communication problems can lead to ill feelings, polarization, and ethnocentrism, which in turn can increase the tendency for misunderstanding, fueled emotional reactions, and escalated conflicts.

Culture clashes during an M&A have been well documented in many case studies, research, and practice. The culture clash process usually unfolds in four stages:

I. Perceived Differences

The process of culture clash innocently begins when managers and employees begin to note differences between the two companies. It becomes interesting when they note differences of style, behavior, and philosophy between the leaders of the two companies. Next, they are exposed to the different ways things are handled, different procedures, and soon realize that all aspects of operations in the two companies are different. If the situation is unmanaged at this stage, differences are likely to be magnified.

II. Magnified Differences

As people spend more time together, the perceived differences between the two firms become sharper. Then, it becomes more polarized over time. When they confront more situations of different behavior, people are fast to draw conclusions about the deeper level of differences in values and beliefs. At this stage, the cultural differences may become sources of conflicts as people do not like the way things are done in the other company, especially the acquired people who need to adapt to procedures and behavior of the other company and change their behavior. This change of processes and procedures is associated with uncertainty about the right way to perform the process task, the successful accomplishment of the task, and the reaction of the supervisors and management of the other company. A causal ambiguity about cause and effect on what leads to successful performance prevails and can result in high anxiety and negative attitudes toward the people of the other company.

III. Stereotypes

Following the generalization process about the other side, people begin to typecast the "others" and feel that "they" are all alike because they all act the same way. This stereotyping is intensified in cross-border mergers or if the two companies are from different regions such as the North and South United States. This process is similar to a process of a tourist visiting another country and arriving to some conclusions about the other society. We regard others' beliefs and habits as strange or eccentric, mainly because they are unlike our own. There is no doubt about it, the Chinese, for instance, are not like Americans! Similarly, this process happens in the contact between people of two companies when people from one company indicate that the other people are "nice" or have "bad manners" and so on.

IV. Putdowns

People from each culture consider themselves normal. Thus, the corollary is that they consider everybody else abnormal. This usually leads to a situation in which the people from each company put down the other culture as having less desirable behavior. "They" are inferior, and "we" are deemed superior. What started as usual conflict escalates especially because the acquirer management adopts superiority syndrome and treats the acquired management and employees as second-class citizens. In such situations, acquired management and employees usually become defensive trying to protect their job, turf, pride, and ways of doing things.

The consequences of the culture clash go beyond anxiety, negative attitudes, and low cooperation between people from both sides. The promised smooth integration never materializes, and key talents and top executives leave the acquired company. Customers become frustrated and look for the competitor for further purchase. Eventually, shareholder value is never created.

Managing the Culture Clash

Planning Stage

The process of culture clash management starts at the planning stage of any M&A before a deal is signed. The aim of this early stage analysis is to analyze the future challenges that will take place during the post-merger integration (PMI) stage and efforts to achieve synergy realization. Actions taken—and not taken—in the planning stage as a deal is being conceived and negotiated set directions whereby the M&A heads down a successful path or veers off toward failure.

The analysis of cultural differences during the planning stage includes identification and assessment of cultural differences between the organization and a candidate for the

M&A. For this purpose, the analysis will be based on all dimensions described in Chapter 6, "Culture and Cultural Differences Analysis," and in various units and functions such as in R&D, marketing, and so on. The aim is to create a database and flow of information that will be used, not only in planning and negotiation, but also after the deal is signed for the PMI stage.

It should be noted that in many M&As, the buyer can have a mindset of a winner and superiority. This mindset can carry over into assumptions that the winning company's culture, as well as procedures and systems, are superior to those of the buying firm. Thus, the previous stages of culture clash can arrive to the "putdown" stage very early.

Therefore, a *joining mindset* should prevail from the early stage of culture analysis through the entire process. At the core of this mindset is the question of whether individuals at the buying company are judging or joining. The difference is that joining builds partnership and collaboration, while judging results in defensiveness and distance. This point of view should reflect the cultural differences analysis. Rather than look at differences only as a problem, you should look at differences also as opportunities for cross-fertilization. This will create an opportunity for cultural synergies and best cultural practices that can be adopted. This will require, of course, the well-managed process of interactions for working through differences. The joint mindset and approach fosters the best conditions for bringing together the best of the two cultures, thereby capturing the competencies of the acquired company.

Negotiation Stage

The beginning of contact between the two cultures starts at the negotiation stage. In fact, here the executives from both sides clearly face cultural differences. It is recommended to explore and discuss cultural differences. This includes discussions on management styles and managerial philosophies. First, it communicates the importance of cultural differences and their roles in the PMI stage to the target firm, too. Second, such discussion can clarify some cultural issues that might be brought up during the planning stage. This discussion has the potential to create an appropriate atmosphere for the negotiation. Furthermore, it creates the atmosphere and necessary conditions for the cultural integration at the PMI stage.

PMI Stage

At this stage, the aim is to create mutual respect for each other's culture. Mutual respect achieves two goals. First, it prevents the putdown syndrome and thus prevents conflicts. Second, it allows a learning process and adoption of best practices of one culture from the other.

The first step will be to educate and create cultural differences awareness on each side. This can be done by various methods such as by top executives of each company speaking about it, by reading materials, and by workshops that include the stages previously described about the development of culture clash. All these methods should include information about the history, people, products, and systems of each company.

The second step aims at clarifying the cultural components of each company. Here analysis done at the planning stage can help. Other methods of learning about the other side can be by show-and-tell meetings. Company newsletters, ceremonies, brochures, videos, websites, and so on can help to describe each company.

The final step, based on the creation of mutual respect, will look for the promotion of cross-fertilization. This can be achieved in joint teams where people from both companies will work together. Each team will be created around similar functions, such as R&D, marketing, human resources, and so on.

Here is an example of a workshop that can help managers and employees from both companies to learn and clarify the differences between the two cultures as well as working through differences. Such a workshop starts with a relatively short presentation about cultural components, cultural differences, and the development of culture clash. The next step is to divide the people of each company into separate groups and give them an assignment about cultural analysis. Each group is asked to describe, first, its own culture, second, the other culture, and finally, how it thinks the people from the other culture perceive its own culture.

This workshop can start with different methods. For example, each group can receive a definition of culture and be asked to answer the preceding three descriptions. A second option can be the use of the seven dimensions described in Chapter 6, and requesting participants in each group to use them for the previous assignments. Another option might be to use the list of items about the way of doing things in any business, such as decision process, reward, and so on, and ask them to describe each company along this list of items.

Usually it takes approximately 20–30 minutes for each group discussing its own culture to realize that it is difficult to reach an agreement among members of the organization on specific cultural components. At this stage, one member in each group indicates that if they have different perceptions of their own culture, probably the other group from the other organization cannot accurately perceive their own culture. Consequently, they understand that they cannot accurately understand the other culture without working with the other people. When all are brought together and are shown one group to the other their summaries about the preceding three assignments, participants understand the misperceptions as well as the need to have an in-depth process of learning about each other.

Other outcomes are the realization that there are many fundamental differences that would have to be worked out if they are to have a chance to successfully integrate the two companies and achieve a successful merger. The workshop creates a constructive forum for an open dialogue on discussing differences and finding a constructive way to reconcile them.

During the following day, after learning more about one another's culture, teams created from people from both sides work on joint assignments. They try to cooperate on achieving common goals as a way of aligning the interests of separate groups. Through these joint assignments, they learn how to work through differences. The process helps participants from both sides to focus on the future tasks of the unit rather than on their parochial interests. This process also helps to adopt features from other cultures to accomplish joint tasks. The guidelines for the task are

- Formulate some major goals for your unit/department.
- Think about the major means to achieve these goals.
- Clarify the main cultural features to best enable the unit to achieve its goals.
- Indicate what cultural features are detrimental for the achievement of goals.
- What cultural components have no impact on the function of the unit?
- What cultural features are essential for the accomplishment of the task?
- What cultural differences might cause conflict?
- What actions are needed to ensure that important components will be retained, adopted, or eliminated?
- What actions should be taken to prevent or minimize the conflicts due to cultural differences?

Tasks at this workshop can actually be about the integration process of participant units from both companies. Each group can concentrate on the integration of their own unit. Through such a workshop, participants can move forward and rebuild the new unit. The process builds cooperation. They will face some conflicts but through the learning experience will have the tools to deal with these conflicts.

References

Boston Consulting Group (BCG). 2010. Cross-border post-merger integration: Understanding and overcoming the challenges. Report. www.bcg.com.

12

COMMUNICATION

Introduction

Communication is a critical activity in M&As because it has a tremendous bearing on value creation. Therefore, communication needs to be managed carefully in a systematic way.

M&As are usually characterized with a high degree of uncertainty especially due to changes and associated ambiguity. At the same time, in an M&A, there are numerous challenges to learning, for instance by knowledge transfer, and to developing a shared view of a new organizational reality. However, an M&A lacks effective communication due to various reasons, such as misinterpretations because of organizational and national cultural differences, that result in conflicts and a lack of trust between the people of the two organizations as well as managers that do not know what and how to communicate and thus might have many "excuses" for avoiding their communication responsibilities.

Communication refers to how messages about the M&A are transferred to others: what is said, how it is said, when it is said, and to whom it is said. In M&As, communication is important to clarify activities and to eventually make people commit to them. The communication can create the difference between whether the merger or acquisition is perceived as an opportunity or a threat.

Although many suggest the use of communication during the post-merger integration (PMI) stage and focus on employees, systematic communication must be used during all stages and to all stakeholders. This chapter discusses plans, issues, and methods for effective communication.

Communications with All Stakeholders

A company has different stakeholders, and each of them needs to be considered in the communication plans. Communication with external stakeholders such as customers, suppliers, investors, financial analysts, and unions, and internal stakeholders such as employees and managers, will be critical, especially when the changes being created might impact them.

Communication should occur both before the M&A actually takes place, throughout the process, and in the PMI phase. Yet, the decision about when to start the communication is not an easy one to make. For example, it might require a balance between the need for secrecy, for instance, to avoid a bidding process, and the beginning of the rumor mill.

It is imperative to find out what each stakeholder wants and needs to know. This can be done through studying all the parties impacted by the deal and the effect of the M&A on them. This can enable communication of the appropriate messages to each stakeholder in a timely manner and the appropriate format. Engagement of stakeholders enables management to gain commitment and reduce resistance. The purpose of engaging stakeholders is to

- Validate your understanding of, and change if necessary, their attitudes to the deal.

- Help to sell the benefits of the deal.

- Help to achieve stakeholder ownership (for example, getting union representatives to undertake parts of the communications to their members).

- Enable the integration plan to highlight early major problems or likely changes (for example, to governmental regulations) that might have an effect on the integration process.

Communicating with External Parties

Press releases are the means to communicate with external parties. Such messages usually focus on the description of the acquirer and the acquired firm, and the motives of the M&A. The idea with the communication is foremost to inform shareholders (and potential shareholders, if the companies are publicly listed) about the M&A. The press releases are a public channel to mass-inform such parties, whereas other types of communication fit better to be personalized and delivered on a one-to-one basis.

In the mass communication of press releases, the information they portray might also reach other parties than those intended: competitors, employees, and so forth. This, in turn, limits what is communicated but also needs to be coordinated with other types of communication directed at different parties. It is not good if employees, for instance, discover in the local news about the M&A, any planned layoff of staff or reorganizations.

In the circumstance of an M&A entailing a publicly traded firm, there are restrictions on when communication is allowed. This results in the balancing act between informing the stock exchange and other parties simultaneously, while ensuring that those other parties do not obtain the information from the public first.

In terms of information to shareholders, this differs intensively between whether the companies are publicly or privately held. If the company is privately owned, owners would have been part of the discussion on the M&A, whereas for publicly traded firms, minority owners would learn about it only through official information. Such information should be concise, be informative, and motivate the M&A. It should also include what lies ahead in terms of integration. The information to shareholders would in the latter part of the M&A be complemented with information regarding integration, changes in locations of businesses, and so forth. Partially, the official information should be regarded as the companies' marketing opportunity. This means that it should talk positively about the companies and the M&A. In addition, it needs to be correct and give a fair view of the transaction. It furthermore needs to be consistent with other communication.

Communication to customers, suppliers, and collaboration partners should be done through multiple channels. For major customers, company visits will be necessary, and the company also needs to train its sales staff in meeting and informing customers in these regards. Such information should include effects on the customer, possible introduction of new contact persons, and information ahead of time on changes. It should be formulated so that it pinpoints the positive effects to the customer, such as the reach for a broader product range, a stronger and healthier supplier, and so on. Similarly, information to collaboration partners should be personal and informal, and be transferred through those various contacts that exist between the company and the collaboration partner. This also requires that it is coordinated, in terms of what is said, who says it, and when between different representatives of the organization. Coherency in content is required, while the level of detailing might differ depending on who receives the information and how it affects that party's work. Suppliers might often act as important partners to a firm, and what is more, represent resources or competencies that the company needs for its products or services. Such suppliers should be treated in a similar way as customers: Information should be personal, informal, and occur between relevant representatives of the firms.

For smaller customers and suppliers, information should be given in writing and complemented with well-informed staff at general sales meeting and so forth. These should answer questions and also give some information about future direction. It is important that the sales and procurement staff are well informed as a consequence because otherwise the communication might be speculative and colored by rumors. Furthermore, it is also important that the staff feels committed to the M&A, so it does not ally with customers or suppliers rather than represent and talk positively about the M&A.

Communication with customers, suppliers, and collaboration partners should continue throughout the process of the M&A. It should be both proactive and reactive in the sense that it should inform before changes occur that target the customer, supplier, or collaboration partner directly or indirectly, and it should answer those questions that arise from these parties. Such questions can occur at any time, and those parties meeting the customers, suppliers, or collaboration partner representatives should be prepared for any such questions at any time.

Other communication with external parties includes the information required by authorities as a consequence of the M&A. This information should be timely, correct, and meet those requirements that the authorities place on the M&A information. There are several examples of how companies can choose entirely different ways of describing their markets in their communication with competition authorities than in their press releases. This is because it is regarded as positive to talk about large market shares with shareholders, while it might actually lead to the discontinuation of the acquisition in the competition authority's evaluation. Because the authorities then rely on different sources to actually determine how the market should be defined, this might backfire to the company.

Communicating with Internal Parties

Communication with internal parties includes the ways messages are given to the employees and representatives of the counterpart. Such information is given for many different reasons: to reduce stress and anxiety, to lead to new ways of working, to enable knowledge transfer, and to unite/highlight cultures and identities. It is also given so that company representatives—both as middle managers in their communication with subordinated staff, and sales, procurement, and marketing staff in their interaction with external parties—transfer a coherent view on the company and the M&A to these parties (see more details later and table with examples).

Communication is vertical in how managers inform employees, but also horizontal in how information is exchanged between employees. It is important that any such information is correct, delivered to employees on a first-hand basis, and also indicates the benefits of the M&A. Informal communication, with a rate of frequency, would help in such communication. Managers' informal efforts and the creation of cooperation increase employees' positive attitude to the M&A. It decreases uncertainty and thereby also several negative effects that might follow from how employees experience the M&A as something negative, or at least as something that is connected with instability during a phase of change. The lack of such communication increases anxiety and decreases trust. Such communication should be marked by honesty, while also highlighting the organizational and individual benefits of the M&A. Furthermore, it should highlight similarities between the firms, so as not to scare the employees. It also needs to be coherent between the media of information and over time.

Communication on integration needs to be started on the day that the deal is announced. It needs to include why the M&A takes place, what synergies are sought, the degree of integration and why it should be done, and a vision of value creation from the M&A. The reason for starting to communicate about the integration from the start is to reduce uncertainty, but also speculations and rumors. People get something constructive to talk about, which is always better than them speculating for better or worse and making decisions based on other parties' speculations. The communication should be a two-way communication. The management team needs to listen to the employees, and the employees should also function as a basis for information that can affect critical decisions. Empowering employees so that they feel confident stating their meaning is important in the communication strategy. A positive communication climate consists of support, openness, participative decision making, trust, confidence, credibility, high-performance goals, adequate information, semantic information difference, and satisfaction with communication.

Communication with employees focused at decreasing their anxiety is proactive in the sense that it is done to reassure and to point to what direction the new organization will take and its actual effects for the people. Communication with people also needs to be considered in a reactive sense. When conflicts occur, or when reorganization makes staff realize that their positions are actually threatened, communication between management and employees is needed. Relative to proactive communication, such communication increasingly needs to be focused on psychological aspects, in-depth, and pursued on a one-to-one person basis.

Communication also needs to occur on horizontal levels, between staff of the acquirer and the acquired party. Such communication, which can take the form of visits, meetings, and face-to-face communication, enables the transfer of knowledge. Communication on both horizontal and vertical levels is also fundamental for the transfer of culture between the organizations. It helps to understand the other party's culture and thereby it is easier to acknowledge it. Hence, communication can be a means both to bring cultures together and to raise awareness of differences. Communication can further be used to transfer identities, both organizational and individual. And it needs to be done to support and accomplish knowledge transfer. Poor communication can undermine any such attempts, as can restrictions to communication. Communication is the start for any change of values, norms, and expectations. Such communication needs to be embedded in meetings, workshops, and so on and occur on local premises, rather than just at meetings in head offices and similar. Communication should be open and informal, so people get to know one another and so that shared values can be shaped between individuals. Open communication also means that confidence rises and that people on cross-organizational levels get to understand one another. This is not less important when different departments are to be integrated.

Other Aspects of Communication

The effect of communication on M&A performance was found to vary in different countries (Weber et al., 2012). Different cultures have different attitudes toward communication. Communication styles range from the close and direct communication in U.S. culture, through the distant understatement and explicit comprehension of British culture, to the indirect, often unspoken, "implicit understanding" of Japanese culture.

In U.S. companies, executives relish the use of first names, establish notice-boards to present mission and vision statements, hold regular meetings at all levels, and publish company newspapers. However, communication between Japanese companies and their UK subsidiaries does not seem as easy or open. French companies seem to entertain little self-doubt, communicating well among themselves but informing acquired executives only on a need-to-know basis, adopting a "colonial attitude." German companies alternate between the stiffly formal and the self-consciously informal. In an empirical investigation of the relationships between communication and M&A overall performance differences, the effects of communication was found to have a different impact on performance of M&A in various countries (Weber et al., 2012). For example, increase in communication was found to have a significant positive association with M&A performance in Japan and Denmark and a significant negative association for German acquirers.

Other considerations can influence communication procedures. In an international M&A, the way of communicating can be changed slightly to become more formal for one of the parties, while it remains as before for the other one (this being the result of how the companies were different in their formalization of communication prior to the acquisition). Suggestion schemes, circles of employees, communication zones, video and frequent meetings among staff were means to both allow for the communication among staff and for management to inform staff. The frequency of meetings subsequently decreased, and ways to communicate changed based on how they were received among employees.

Another issue in communication in the cross-border M&A is the language to be chosen as the corporate language, provided that the companies are not located in countries with similar language. The introduction of a corporate language can counteract integration for those who need to adjust, and it becomes important to figure out a language integration plan as a consequence. In addition, different cultures have different ways of communicating, with a range from direct communication to an implicit one, focus on formalities and less formal styles. Some studies on international M&As describe how there are national differences in terms of formality/informality, openness/control, and directness of communication (Pitkenthly, R., Faulkner, D., and Child, J. 2003). For example, Japanese firms acted on a need-to-know basis; U.S. firms were formal but open; French companies were more top-down controlled; whereas German firms were formal in a bottom-up communication, while less so from the parent company to the subsidiaries.

Another specific type of M&A is the acquisition of technology-intensive firms. In such acquisitions, communication is important to accomplish knowledge transfer. This also draws attention to the role of communication for tacit as well as explicit knowledge. Although the latter can be communicated through manuals and other types of written, formalized communication, tacit knowledge transfer requires face-to-face interaction, in-depth communication, and actions as part of the communication. Company visits and meetings help in such endeavors.

Managing Communication

There are several key elements for establishing effective communication strategy and process:

- Establish communication principles.

- Establish fit between management messages and stakeholders' needs.

- Develop a communication plan.

- Choose effective communication media.

- Control and evaluate the effects of communication and revise accordingly.

I. Communication Principles

Communication should be guided by principles agreed on by management. Examples of such principles follow:

- Messages should represent the mission, values, strategic objectives, and plans of the merger and integration process.

- **Timely**—All messages should be made as early as possible.

- **Relevance**—Although communication is used by management to announce and promote important issues, it should also focus on what people want to know.

- **Honest and balanced**—Stakeholders should be made aware of the limits as well as opportunities. Research shows that honesty does pay. A large gap between communication and reality will lower credibility of leadership and will cause frustration that will impact performance of individuals and the merger.

- **Consistency**—The important messages should be consistent through various channels. Consistency is important not only because some people misinterpret some announcements, or did not get all aspects, but also because if contradictory or not consistent, people will not feel that messages can be trusted.

II. Fit Between Messages and Recipient's Needs

Executives, and consultants, think that it is important to communicate the vision for the merged organization, strategic benefits of the merger, changes in organizational structure and product lines, and so on. They are right. However, most managers and employees involved in an M&A, especially those in the acquired company, want to hear about the impact that such processes as PMI have on them. They may care about the strategic decisions and their company but usually are more concerned about changes in their jobs, provisions for layoffs, changes in benefits and compensations, their autonomy, how to be successful in the new environment, greater or fewer career opportunities, and the like. People will remain unsettled until details and information about "me" issues are communicated. It should be noted that the sooner people get answers about these issues, the sooner they can move on and contribute to the success of the M&A.

III. Communication Plan

The communication plan's main objective is to ensure that the appropriate communications are provided to all stakeholders at the right time. Without such planning, for instance, insufficient communication from executives can lead other managers to stall the integration process. When your stakeholders—employees, customers, suppliers, and investors—spend time worrying and wondering, they are not producing, buying, supplying, or investing.

A good communication plan can break down barriers to change and secure people's buy-in. Obviously, the communication process evolves as the M&A goes through various stages. For example, the first stage will aim at awareness building in which strategic plans will be linked to different stages.

The plan should include the following:

- The goals behind the messages that will be communicated. These messages are not only for explaining new tasks following the merger. For example, messages can aim to prevent uncertainty among key talents that might otherwise not remain in the company.
- The target stakeholder of each message.
- The person that is best for each message. For example, in some cases, the CFO communicates to financial analysts rather than the CEO.
- The most effective media for each message.
- The timing and frequency of specific messages.

Table 12.1 illustrates examples of main components of a communication plan with examples of various stakeholders.

Table 12.1 The Main Components of a Communication Plan with Various Stakeholders

To Whom	Why	What	How	Who	When and How Often
Stakeholders	Objectives	Key Messages	Media	Accountability to deliver	Timing
Senior Managers					
Middle Managers					
Employees					
Shareholders					
Customers					
Suppliers					
Unions					
Community					

IV. Effective Media Channels

See the next section.

V. Effectiveness of Communication

Mechanisms for two-way feedback should be developed and used in all M&A stages. The control systems should focus on feedback from various stakeholders' reactions as well as on specific goals, milestones, and any deviation from original planning. For example, one goal of communication is to reduce uncertainty and ambiguity. These should be evaluated throughout the process.

Methods and Channels of Communication

Table 12.1 points to how communication should be consistent, targeted, continue over time, and often use several channels. The appropriate channel for communication can prevent problems such as distress. Communicating via e-mail, faxes, or even the media can make people resist the merger or its integration, and it also makes them question the leaders and their intentions. Hence, it is important to choose a method and channel of communication wisely.

At large, a distinction should be made between mass communication to reach parties at the same time with the same information, and informal, person-to-person communication with opportunities to reflect and form the message to fit the receiver. In both cases, communication should be consistent between sources, and it should be followed up when new changes are introduced. There is also a major difference between communication to inform and communication to, for instance, transfer identities, integrate cultures, or transfer knowledge. Those latter forms of communication need to be directed from the start and later increasingly rely on those parties that are the carriers of the identities, cultures, or knowledge.

For mass communication, channels include web pages, press releases, news media, and general meetings. Often several such channels are used in parallel, and the communication plan should then ensure that the same information is given in spite of the channel. This further requires internal coordination among marketing, finance, and top management, for instance, as the responsibility for the information normally relies on those different parties.

Communication aimed to inform important customers, suppliers, collaboration partners, and employees should be much more integrated in the ordinary interaction between parties, while also adding to it. Channels here include written texts, complemented with company visits, person-to-person talks, and less conventional channels. Unconventional methods and channels to communicate include courses, workshops, and psychological counselling. The creation of opportunities for staff to meet and ask questions, establish trust among them through joint projects, and so on, are increasingly important as methods to handle changes of cultures and identities, let alone the transfer of knowledge. Here, the unit of communication shifts to become determined by those parties that interact, while guided by management. The transfer of knowledge is the communication that needs to be the most informalized and based on local-level interaction, especially when it comes to tacit knowledge. Such communication also needs to be allowed to take time and be adjusted to those parties involved.

References

Pitkenthly, R., Faulkner, D., and Child, J. (2003). Integrating acquisitions. *Advances in Mergers & Acquisitions*, 2, 27-57.

Weber, Y., Rachman-Moore, D., and Tarba, S. Y. (2012). Human resource practices during post-merger conflict and merger performance. *International Journal of Cross-Cultural Management*, 12 (1), 73-99.

13

INTEGRATION APPROACHES

Introduction

The creation of value in the M&A by exploitation of synergy requires the integration of activities, and sometimes facilities, of both companies. This process that involves various ways of contact between managers and employees of the two companies usually creates both culture clash and resistance of the acquired managers to the related process of autonomy removal. This chapter deals with the challenges of these processes.

Integration and Culture Clash

The management literature in recent years emphasizes first and foremost the importance of the fit between the two management cultures involved in the merger to the success of the post-merger integration (PMI) process. If great differences exist between the two cultures, a conflict arises between the two groups of executives, and it becomes difficult to bring about the successful integration of the two firms.

The level of contact between the two cultures, due to integration process activities, can affect the level of the conflict created during the M&A. The contact between the two firms produced by the integration results in a culture clash because it exposes the belief and value systems of the two teams to each other and makes the differences salient. At higher levels of integration, a higher level of contact between people of both organizations necessarily occurs. The acquiring management team frequently imposes more of the features of its culture on the acquired management team. This is because higher level of contact between the cultures emphasizes cultural differences and gives the dominant management culture many more opportunities to dictate to the governed management, increasing friction and conflict. It should be noted that this will not always be the acquiring company's culture.

The level of contact increases as the level of integration between the managements increases. This elicits further conflict because it underscores the cultural differences and lowers commitment and cooperation. The culture clash, the level of integration, and the ensuing human resource problems can adversely affect the realization of value creation from an acquisition.

Generally, the acquiring company rarely allows the acquired firm full autonomy, but when the autonomy is too restricted, the acquired management team might feel more dominated, which tends to create more clashes within the new organization.[1] Therefore, in some cases, companies might try to minimize problems of incompatibility by minimizing their interactions with their partners and allowing them more autonomy. When one of the company's management team has a positive view of the other, and the organizational fit is high, they might be willing to give up their autonomy and even to adopt their culture.

Trade-Off Between Integration and Synergy Exploitation

Post-acquisition integration and resource reconfiguration are necessary to exploit potential synergies between the acquired and acquiring firms. But the loss of autonomy that often accompanies the integration process can be detrimental to acquisition performance. Moreover, effective integration of the target firm entails a substantial commitment of managerial resources on the part of the buying company, a requirement that can distract the acquirer from its own core business.

The dilemma of post-acquisition integration versus synergy potential exploitation in M&A deals is particularly salient in the acquisition of hi-tech firms. These deals are often motivated by the desire to obtain and transfer tacit and socially complex knowledge-based resources. Because these forms of knowledge are difficult to transfer (see Chapter 5, "Synergy Potential and Realization"), a high degree of post-acquisition integration can be required to realize the anticipated benefits of these acquisitions. Yet integration can ultimately lead to the destruction of the acquired firm's knowledge-based resources through employee turnover and disruption of organization routines. An additional problem is that external parties have difficulty observing tacit and socially complex knowledge. Initially, acquirers might have poor information about where valuable knowledge resides in the acquired firm and about the type of that knowledge. As a result, the management of the acquiring company is liable to make ineffective or inadequate decisions about the post-acquisition integration approach to be implemented.

Autonomy appears to be an important means of protecting the acquired hi-tech firms' technologies and capabilities during acquisition implementation. It can be manifested at different levels and in different forms. Retaining the acquired firm's valuable knowledge is clearly a critical precursor to the subsequent transfer of the acquired firm's technologies and capabilities. In particular, the more tacit and socially complex the knowledge is, the more apparent is the importance of allowing the acquired organization a considerable degree of autonomy to protect the social organizational context.

Cultural Differences and Levels of Integration

There are inconsistent findings about the role of cultural difference in the success of international M&As (Rotting, Reus, and Tarba, 2013; Weber and Tarba, 2013). Research on domestic M&As consistently shows that corporate culture clash is detrimental to PMI and to merger effectiveness (Datta, 1991; Lubatkin et al., 1994, Weber, 1996). However, although some studies point out the negative effect of national culture on the success of international M&As (Datta and Puia, 1995), other findings show that the level of cultural conflict varies in different international combinations (Very, Lubatkin, Calori, and Veiga, 1997), and greater differences in national culture might be positively related to performance (Morosini et al., 1998).

It is not clear how national culture interacts with organizational culture and what might be the effect of this interaction on M&A performance.

The research study (Very, Lubatkin, Calori, and Veiga, 1997) has found that a greater need for uncertainty avoidance and greater acceptance of power distance (French versus British acquirers) were associated with a higher level of integration (more centralized control), but where cultural difference was positively related to performance, integration did not show any significant relationship with performance (Morosini et al., 1998). Another study shows that the relationship between the degree of integration and the cooperation of the acquired top management team with the acquiring top managers was negative in international mergers (Weber et al., 1996). Other interesting findings show that differences between nations pursuing M&A rather than cultural differences were associated with the level of integration (Child et al., 2000; Pitkethly, Faulkner, and Child, 2003). For example, American acquirers tended to implement a high level of integration of subsidiaries, whereas Japanese and German companies preferred low levels of integration. French companies inclined to an average level of integration. Other studies did not find relationship between cultural differences and level of integration (Datta, 1991; Larsson & Finkelstein, 1999).

These findings show that cultural differences, whether organizational or national, show different relationships with the level of integration and with M&A performance. Yet, the direction of this relationship is not clear and its effect on performance is vague. The review of literature indicates that most studies investigated two independent variables as critical to M&A performance: cultural differences (organizational culture in a domestic M&A and national culture in a cross-border M&A) and level of integration (Rotting, Reus, and Tarba, 2013; Weber, Tarba, and Reichel, 2009). But findings are not consistent and sometimes they are contradictory, indicating that the relationship between these important variables and M&A performance is complex and that a better framework than the existing one is required to explain it. The review of literature findings also raises some important issues and questions. First, there is a relationship between level of integration and cultural differences, whether national or organizational, which can affect the M&A performance. Second, it is not clear whether only the extent of the difference between cultures is important or also its direction. For instance, does higher uncertainty avoidance of the acquirer versus the acquired company have the same effect as lower uncertainty avoidance? Third, given that different national cultures use different levels of integration, what are the cultural features that influence the level of integration?

In sum, the extent of the cultural differences and the level of integration is not sufficient to explain M&A performance. The PMI process is a complex phenomenon that requires a better conceptualization than the simple linear relationship suggested by the studies reviewed earlier. The following sections suggest additional factors and a configurational fit for the PMI.

M&A Performance and Integration Approaches

It is generally agreed that merging firms transfer capabilities, cut costs, and achieve synergy by integrating management decision making as well as departments and functions such as marketing, inventory, IT, and others. The integration can yield positive M&A performance.

Integration, however, is an interactive and gradual process in which individuals from two organizations must learn to work together and cooperate. "Creating an atmosphere that can support it [the integration] is the real challenge" (Haspeslagh and Jemison, 1991). To achieve effective PMI, the top acquiring management typically intervenes in the decision-making process of the acquired management team and imposes standards, rules, and expectations on it. The intended integration may affect the commitment of the top acquired management to the acquiring team and its cooperation with it. The intervention of the top acquiring management team in the decision-making results of the acquired management represents a loss of autonomy that elicits tensions and negative attitudes toward the merger.

There is an explicit trade-off between high and low levels of integration. High levels of integration can be needed to exploit high levels of synergy, but a high level of integration can cause human resource problems that have the potential to destroy the value of the acquired firm and increase costs to an extent that offsets the benefits expected from the merger. Understanding this trade-off can account for the conflicting findings about the relationships between integration (or autonomy removal) and merger performance. For example, some studies found that integration is positively associated with performance (Larsson and Finkelstein, 1999; Weber, 1996), whereas others found integration to be non-significant in domestic (Datta, 1991) and international M&A (Morosini et al., 1998).

In yet another study it was found that performance was negatively related to integration (formal control over operational procedures) in international M&A (Calori, Lubatkin, & Very, 1994). And others found that found that the greater the level of integration (autonomy removal through the interventions of the acquiring top management in the decision process of the acquired top management) the greater the turnover of the acquired top managers (Lubatkin, Schweiger, and Weber, 1999). Loss of these executives viewed as a serious reduction in valuable resources, thereby decreasing the value of the firm acquired. Indeed, it was found that the greater the rate of turnover of top executives, the lower is the performance of the acquiring firm (Hambrick & Cannella, 1993).

The framework suggested here indicates that acquirers should consider not only the synergy potential and implementation difficulties that are due to cultural differences but also their preferences for level of integration based on their cultural characteristics and traits, where they can be most effective within the integration approach chosen for the M&A. By acting in this manner, managers of the acquirer have the highest chance of doing best what they prefer and know to do. Acquirers, therefore, choose the right level of integration within their integration approach. For example, although two acquirers from different countries might both choose absorption, they might differ with respect to their ideal type of absorption (for example, partial) and to their level of integration, depending on their national cultural dimensions. Each acquirer can achieve optimum M&A performance with different levels of integration. Following the suggested framework, each company would also consider its own national dimensions and preferences. Thus, whereas one adopts the full level of integration according to its chosen approach (for instance, full absorption), the other acquirer might use a different level of integration even if it opts for the same integration approach (absorption), but from the point of view that the level of integration absorption will be partial.

With respect to cultural differences and cultural dimensions, it is argued here that the varied cultural dimensions during integration enable the members of the organization to use diverse cultural materials selectively. The appropriation of certain cultural traits and the holding back of others enables the acquiring management to define and strive toward its "ideal cultural type"—which essentially reflects the kind of integration it aspires to. Thus, selective cultural dimensions and traits might cause less conflict. By identifying and adopting the required cultural traits, the acquired management can feel more confident about cultural integration and accept further dimensions of acquirer culture at later stages of the integration.

The choices to be made extend to both the integration approach and level of integration because in each approach an inadequate level of integration, whether too much or too little, can be detrimental to performance. An M&A that approximates its ideal types of integration approach and level of integration is expected to be more effective than an M&A that does not do so. Put differently, the closer an acquirer comes to its ideal type, that is, to the right level of integration within the approach chosen for specific synergy potential, cultural difference, and cultural dimensions, the higher the performance of the merger will be.

A Framework for Integration Approach Choice

In light of the previous findings and studies review, a framework for integration approaches based on the work of Weber, Tarba, and Reichel (2009) is presented. Figure 13.1 presents the integration approach choices as the dependent variable affected by synergy potential, cultural differences, and cultural specific dimensions (either national or organizational).

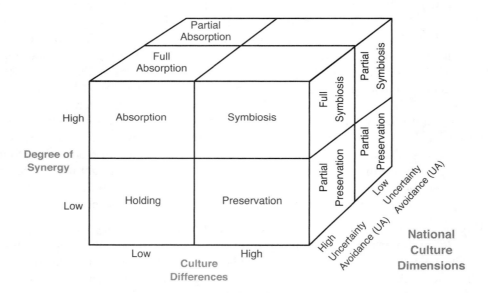

Figure 13.1   Integration Approaches, Cultural Differences,
and National Cultural Dimensions (for example,
only uncertainty avoidance culture dimension is presented)

The *absorption* approach, which requires a high level of integration and thus the lowest autonomy for the acquired management, is recommended for achieving a high level of synergy when the level of cultural differences is low. *Preservation*, which reflects the lowest level of integration and therefore the highest autonomy for the acquired management, is recommended for low synergy potential and high cultural differences. *Symbiosis*, with moderate levels of synergy and cultural differences, reflects a moderate level of integration.

Weber, Reichel, and Tarba (2006) suggested that an early focus on strategic capabilities must be preserved to the extent that these capabilities depend on maintaining cultural differences. Because cultural differences can be of critical importance, depending on the synergy potential, they should be considered when deciding on the choice of integration approach. This is exactly what the framework recommends, that is, to include both synergy potential and cultural differences as major determinants of the integration approach.

The framework suggests that Hofstede's national cultural dimensions and/or GLOBE dimensions should serve as a third determinant of integration approach. Cultural dimensions include both national cultural dimensions and organizational cultural dimensions that are widely used and appear to have different effects on integration and M&A performance.

Furthermore, it is important to note that the assumption about cultural distance symmetry has no empirical support. According to this assumption, a British firm acquiring a French firm is faced with the same cultural distance as a French firm acquiring a British one, so the effects of the cultural dimension on the level of integration and on performance is the same. However, no studies have demonstrated such symmetry. On the contrary, it was found that French acquirers (high power distance and uncertainty avoidance [UA]) exerted greater centralized formal control, that is, higher levels of integration, over the strategy and operations of their acquired businesses than did British acquirers (lower UA), who leaned toward informal communication and cooperation, requiring lower levels of formal integration. The differential exercise of control mechanisms was found to correlate with acquisition performance (Calori et al., 1994).

Moreover, other recent findings indicate that it is not only corporate (organizational) cultural differences that affect decisions about the level of integration but also differences between national cultures (Weber, Tarba, and Reichel, 2009). It was found that acquirers of UK companies from different nations used different levels of integration, control, and practices after the acquisition (Child et al., 2000). Finally, given recent evidence that different national managerial groups have dissimilar attitudinal preferences toward M&As with foreign partners, the different national cultural dimensions can be important factors in managerial preferences for integration approaches based on cultural differences and cultural dimensions (Cartwright and Price, 2003). These findings suggest that above and beyond cultural distance, the organizational and national culture dimensions of the acquirer have a bearing on the acquirer's choice of level of integration and eventually on merger success. And all these are recommendations derived from the previously described framework and figure.

Acquirers from countries that present relatively high UA traits make great efforts to avoid conflicts and prefer formal processes and procedures. Therefore, according to the framework and the previous cube, their recommended *preservation* approach is characterized by lower autonomy for the acquired management and a higher level of integration (*partial preservation*) than the *full preservation* adopted by acquirers with lower UA. Because the *preservation* approach is characterized by low levels of integration, a relatively small increase in integration is not likely to cause much conflict. Similarly, using the *absorption* approach, acquirers with low UA exercise lower levels of integrations (*partial absorption*) with fewer formal procedures and processes than acquirers with high UA (*full Absorption*).

Finally, the effect of culture on M&A integration can be understood by examining the ways in which members of the organizations that partnered in the merger integrate their different cultural understanding into the new organization. An important choice involves the selection from an array of cultural dimensions of those cultural traits that can facilitate the implementation of the integration process, such as UA, or innovation, and action orientation (see Chapter 6, "Culture and Cultural Differences Analysis").

References

Calori, R., Lubatkin, M., and Very, P. (1994). Control mechanisms in cross-border acquisitions: An international comparison. *Organization Studies*, 15, 361–379.

Cartwright, S. and Price, F. (2003). Managerial preferences in international merger and acquisition partners revisited: How are they influenced? *Advances in Mergers and Acquisitions*, 2, 81–95.

Child, J., Faulkner, D., and Pitkethly, R. (2000). Foreign direct investment in the UK 1985–1994: The impact on domestic management practice. *Journal of Management Studies*, 37 (1), 141–166.

Datta, D. (1991). Organizational fit and acquisition performance: Effects of post-acquisition integration. *Strategic Management Journal*, 12, 281–297.

Datta, D. K. and Puia, G. (1995). Cross-border acquisitions: An examination of the influence of relatedness and cultural fit on shareholder value creation in U.S. acquiring firms. *Management International Review*, 35 (4), 337-359.

Hambrick, D.C. and Cannella, A. A., Jr . (1993). Relative standing: A framework for under- standing departures of acquired executives. *Academy of Management Journal*, 36(4), 733–762.

Haspeslagh, P. C. and Jemison, D. B. (1991). *Managing acquisitions: Creating value through corporate renewal*. New York: Free Press.

Larsson, R. and Finkelstein, S. (1999). Integrating strategic, organizational, and human resource perspectives on mergers and acquisitions: A case survey of synergy realization. *Organization Science*, 10 (1), 1–26.

Lubatkin, M., Calori, R., Very, P., and Veiga, J. (1998). Managing mergers across borders: A two nation exploration of a nationally bound administrative heritage. *Organization Science*, 9(6), 670–684.

Lubatkin, M., Schweiger, D., and Weber, Y. (1999). Top management turnover in related M&A's: An additional test of the theory of relative standing. *Journal of Management*, 25 (1), 55–73.

Morosini, P., Shane, S., and Singh, H. (1998). National cultural distance and cross-border acquisition performance. *Journal of International Business Studies*, 29 (1), 137-158.

Pitkethly, R., Faulkner, D., and Child, J. (2003). Integrating acquisitions. *Advances in Mergers and Acquisitions*, 2, 27–57.

Rottig, D., Reus, T., and Tarba, S.Y. (2013). The impact of culture on mergers and acquisitions: 30 years of research. *Advances In Mergers and Acquisitions*, 12, 135-173.

Very, P., Lubatkin, M., Calori, R., and Veiga, J. (1997). Relative standing and the performance of recently acquired European firms. *Strategic Management Journal*, 18 (8), 593-614.

Weber, Y. (1996). Corporate culture fit and performance in mergers and acquisitions. *Human Relations*, 49 (9), 1181–1202.

Weber, Y., Tarba, S.Y., and Reichel, A. (2009). International mergers and acquisitions performance revisited - The role of cultural distance and post-acquisition integration approach implementation. *Advances in Mergers and Acquisitions*, 8, 1-18.

Weber, Y., Reichel, A., and Tarba, S.Y. (2006). International mergers and acquisitions performance: Acquirer nationality and integration approaches. *Best Paper Proceedings of Academy of Management*.

Weber, Y., Tarba, S.Y., and Reichel, A. (2011). International mergers and acquisitions performance: Acquirer nationality and integration approaches. *International Studies of Management & Organization*, 41 (3), 9-24.

Weber, Y., Shenkar, O., and Raveh, A. (1996). National and corporate culture fit in mergers/acquisitions: An exploratory study. *Management Science*, 42 (8), 1215-1227.

Weber, Y. and Tarba, S.Y. (2013). Sociocultural integration in mergers and acquisitions – New perspectives. *Thunderbird International Business Review*, 55 (4), 327-331.

Weber, Y. and Schweiger, D. (1992).Top management culture in mergers and acquisitions: A lesson in anthropology. *The International Journal of Conflict Management*, 3(4), 285–302.

14

HUMAN CAPITAL ISSUES AND PRACTICES

Plenty of attention from executives, employees, and consultants is paid to the financial, legal, and operational elements of the M&A. But, executives who have been through an M&A, especially the post-merger integration (PMI) process, now recognize that in today's economy, the management of the human capital side of change is the real key to creation of value in the M&A. Recent studies consistently show that more than 50 percent of experienced executives think that the human factor is critical for successful integration of the two parties in M&A. However, the combination of culture clash and ill-conceived HR integration strategy is one of the most common reasons for the high failure rate of the M&A. The purpose of this chapter is to articulate a systematic, people-oriented approach for effective implementation of the M&A from the planning stage to integration at the PMI stage. Moreover, HR practices can create capabilities and knowledge that improve competitive advantages and performance of companies engaged in multiple M&As.

The Human Factor

The integration of two organizations is an interactive and gradual process in which managers and employees from both companies have to learn to work together and cooperate in the sharing resources process and transfer of resources and capabilities. The success of the integration process depends on cooperation between managers and employees of both firms and on the ability to address conflicts and various human resource problems. As was indicated in previous chapters, transferring and integrating such resources during PMI is difficult because of cultural differences that create conflict, communication problems, employee resistance, and turnover of acquired talent and executives. First, this chapter develops an understanding of the role of HR practices in the conflict situation that arise during the post-merger process. Second, it provides the tools and practices to overcome those conflicts during the PMI stage.

The management of human capital in the M&A, based upon the high failure rates of M&As, appears to be a somewhat neglected issue during various stages of the deal. It seems that executives see the human factor as too soft and therefore hard to manage. It is much easier to deal with numbers about the M&A value and price, opportunity to save money from operational integration, and so on. Thus, because the focus is usually on finance, accounting, and manufacturing which can be relatively easy to measure, the human side is neglected from M&A consideration until after the deal is signed. Top managers, including HR managers, are not aware about the possibility to measure cultural differences and predict culture clash and HR challenges before the deal is signed. Therefore, HR managers are usually not involved in planning and negotiation stages. In some cases, there is a lack of awareness that people issues are critical. As a result, for most top management teams that are involved in M&A, there is no framework or any model that serves as a tool to systematically manage human capital issues.

The Effects of Cultural Differences and Level of Integration on Behavior in an M&A

The main factors that influence the behavior of people in an M&A are culture clash, the level of integration of the two companies, and the nature of contact (friendliness). The effects of the level of integration that is, in fact, removal of autonomy from acquired managers can occur also when the culture of the two companies is similar. This section elaborates on both.

Culture Clash Effects on Behavior

The culture clash evolution and stages that result in communication problems, fuel emotional reaction, and escalate conflicts are described in Chapter 11, "Management of Culture Clash." The conflict that results from cultural differences in an M&A is characterized by

- Tension, distrust, and annoyance mainly on the part of the acquired people in working with the acquiring managers

- Negative attitudes on the part of the acquired people toward both the acquiring organization and its management

- Negative attitudes toward cooperating with the management and employees of the acquiring company

The success or failure of M&A depends not only on how much synergy is potentially available from the combination but, more important, on whether the synergy can actually be realized through effective integration. Realizing synergies in an M&A can be an arduous and difficult task, and depends to a large extent on the commitment and cooperation of the acquired people.

Commitment can be defined as the willingness to exert effort on behalf of the organization and the desire to maintain membership in it. The level of commitment is affected by the acquired people's attitude toward the new organization and its level of tension. Therefore, the relationships of tension and negative attitudes of the acquired people toward the new organization and commitment can be summarized as follows: The greater the tension and the more negative the attitudes of the acquired people toward the new organization, the lower is their commitment to the M&A and its success.

Furthermore, noncooperative behavior in the M&A can result from acquired people's negative attitudes toward the act of cooperating with the acquiring people. A negative attitude toward the M&A (the object) can also lead to noncooperative behavior on the part of the acquired people. Finally, low levels of commitment are found to be associated with high rates of voluntary turnover. Thus, the culture clash and its behavioral consequences lead not only to poor performance of the acquired people, but also to turnover of key talents and top executives. This, in turn, was found by empirical studies to lead to poor performance of the buying company after the merger (Lubatkin et al., 1999).

Level of Integration Effects on Behavior

Merging firms cut costs and achieve synergy by integrating similar departments and functions, such as marketing, inventory, and so forth. To achieve that integration, acquiring management typically intervenes in the decision-making process of the acquired management and imposes standards, rules, and expectations on them. M&As vary in their intended level of integration. The higher the intended integration, the more effort the acquiring firm must make to control and coordinate decisions and activities, not only by determining goals for the acquired company, but also by other activities such as generating alternative solutions to strategic problems and making crucial choices.

Findings from M&A studies show that the more members of two cultures come into contact and the more contacts they have per period of time, the greater the ability of the dominant culture to expose the weaker one to its own features or to impose them on it, and the greater the subsequent potential for conflict (Weber and Drori, 2011). This section contends that in M&As, the degree of contact between the acquired and the acquiring cultures and the extent to which the weaker culture is dominated by the stronger are determined by the level of integration of the two organizations and their people.

The level of integration, and the implied removal of autonomy from acquired management, influences emotions and attitudes that affect acquired top managers' commitment to and cooperation with the acquiring management. This can be expected to happen in two ways. One is through a main effect that could occur even where the cultures of the two companies are relatively similar! For many top executives who have previously managed independent operations, superimposed authority following the M&A is bound to be objectionable. The loss of autonomy through the intervention of the acquiring management in the acquired management decision making can be expected to evoke tension and negative attitudes toward the merger.

In addition to its main effect, the level of integration can have an interaction effect with cultural differences. The integration of two firms requires contact (not necessarily physical) in the decision-making process between the two management groups. This contact can elicit conflict because it exposes the belief systems of the two teams to each other and makes the differences salient. Furthermore, at higher levels of integration, the acquiring firm imposes more of its beliefs and values on the acquired management; this imposition can also contribute to the salience of any cultural differences and to their ability to cause conflict and tension and to lower commitment and cooperation.

As was indicated in Chapter 6, "Culture and Cultural Differences Analysis," the effects of cultural differences will vary in the M&A with different integration approaches. The impact will be felt most strongly in absorption types (high synergy, low cultural differences, and low autonomy) in which integration brings full consolidation of the two cultures. It will be felt least in a preservation approach in which the source of the acquired benefits remains almost intact.

Nature of Contact

The nature of the contact, whether it is friendly or hostile, is determined by the extent to which top management has a free choice prior to the merger or acquisition in having the other company as a partner. M&A literature recognizes that whether an acquisition is friendly or hostile can influence the amount of conflict between acquiring and acquired executives (Gomes, Angwin, Weber, and Tarba, 2013). For example, the friendliness of the negotiations affects the motivation, commitment, and cooperation of the acquired top management team during the PMI process. Unfriendly takeovers are likely to promote more conflicts than voluntary M&As as the unfriendliness of the purchase poses an immediate threat and presages a battlefield mentality.

Although cultural differences are a source of conflict even in friendly M&As, their effects are likely to be much worse in unfriendly takeovers. An unfriendly takeover is likely to provoke resistance on the part of the acquired management to the dominant firm's culture, especially if the two are different; and the concomitant hostility can prevent friendly exploration of cultural similarities and resolution of cultural differences, which can further undermine the integration process in M&As.

HR Issues, Implications, and Actions at M&A Stages

It is apparent that HR and organizational issues have never received the level of attention from top managers that they should. The usual case is that the HR issues are left out until it is too late. For example, in most M&As, HR departments are never consulted until well after the due diligence phase is completed—too late for them to issue effective warnings about key human capital risks and liabilities. Yet, there are findings that show the financial contribution of HR activities in various countries, as well as positive relationships between early involvement of HR, due diligence with respect to cultural differences, and HR policies. Most experienced executives in an M&A indicate that "people" issues will have much higher priority in the future than they had in the past. Table 14.1 shows the importance of HR activities in various stages.

Table 14.1   Importance of HR at M&A Stages

HR Issues in Various Activities	Planning Stage	Negotiation Stage	Implementation Stage PMI
Cultural Difference	V V V	V V	V V V
Communication	V V	---	V V V
Executive Leadership Team	V V	---	---
Transition Management Structure	---	---	V V V
Staffing, Retainment, Selection	V	V	V V V
Organizational Structure	---	---	V V V
Pay and Reward Systems	V	V	V V V
Retirement and Benefits	V	V	V V V
Training and Learning	---	---	V V V

Scholars and consultants (Weber and Tarba, 2010 and 2012) see major roles of HR in M&As as *strategic partner* (strategic HR considerations), *administrative expert* (management of organizational structure and policies), *employee champion* (leadership, motivation, retaining of key talents, and other related issues), and *change agent* (culture integration, dealing with conflicts). These roles are related and will be discussed at each M&A stage.

Planning Stage

The main role of the HR department at this early stage is of the strategic partner who helps in the screening process and selecting the target company, using such tools as cultural differences assessment and appraisal of key talents and top executives of the target firm. Cultural assessment involves articulation of all cultural dimensions of both companies as well as other characteristics of culture (see Chapter 6). The selection process also considers issues of labor relations. In some international mergers, this issue can be a "killing" factor for specific target companies given expected difficulties with unions and employees.

During the due diligence process, HR managers also have the role of employee champion and change agent and thus have to collect data on various areas about the target company such as its culture, rewards, appraisal, training, benefits, and more. They also have to consider a list of possible integration problem areas. HR managers look at, among other things, such issues as potential liabilities for retiree medical benefits and severance pay obligations. Similarly, any commitment to employees and managers following a merger should be investigated, such as a parachute for top executives. In international mergers, or when the company diversifies into different industries, HR must check issues of the competitive labor market for talent, appropriate mix of direct and incentive compensation, rewards that reinforce the business strategy and cultural components, performance measures that affect rewards, and more.

At this stage, the process also creates a great deal of uncertainty for managers and employees of both buying and target companies, which can result in stress and anxiety that result in higher absenteeism, health problems, and lower productivity and commitment to both organizations. This usually happens because employees often learn through the grapevine and newspapers that their company is considering an M&A. It is a time when employees look for information, but unfortunately, it is also a time when communication is greatly restricted. Thus, the rumor mill, which rarely spreads accurate information, heats up during this stage and needlessly fuels employees' concern and stress. Here the HR managers are both employee champion and change agent and have to create a communication plan that articulates communication philosophy, media, type of information to communicate, and who to communicate with (for more details see Chapter 12, "Communication").

When the process enters a more intensive stage right after signing the letter of intention (LOI), the buying company will establish the executive team (see Chapter 13, "Integration Approaches") that will guide the M&A process. Here the HR department becomes the administrative expert and assists in the setup of the transition and integration team, and the selection of the leader and managers to be part of this team. It will clarify the new leadership roles and organizational structure. In many cases, especially in an M&A that is characterized by paying high premium for the buying company, top executives expect urgent integration that will lead quickly to positive performance. Here the HR department can help to maintain a realistic expectation as to the pace of change.

Negotiation Stage

All issues from the planning stage, data collected, and assessments made by HR managers can be used for the negotiation of price and terms. Furthermore, the negotiation stage should be used for both collecting more data and to confirm understandings and assessments made at the planning stage.

At this stage, HR managers are also strategic partners, as well as employee champions and change agents. The HR department, especially in an organization that grows through the M&A, will provide training programs in negotiation and help its top executives to improve their negotiation skills. Also, among other things, HR managers will give each member of the negotiation team a list of questions about culture that can be used to check personally with the members of the negotiation team of the other company. After the meeting, each member of the team will fill out a questionnaire based on the dimensions and items presented in Chapter 6. At the HR department, the results of the questionnaire will be summarized and sent to each member of the negotiation team to be used in further negotiation meetings to facilitate the negotiation process and achieve best possible results. For example, data and assessment can be used to create "chemistry" (see Chapter 8, "Selection of Target and Negotiation Process"), facilitate a win-win situation, add a member to the team who can create better contact with the other party's team, and so on. Moreover, using the cultural differences evaluation can help to predict challenges and problems during the integration process. It can help in assessing costs, time to achieve synergy, and the uncertainty in realizing some of the planned synergy. All this information can be used to drive the price down. Later, these results, together with previous analysis will be used in the implementation stage for the integration process.

Trust-building starts at the negotiation stage, and HR managers have to provide tools for the negotiation team for creating and maintaining trust. These, of course, will include the assessment of cultural differences, appropriate behavior, and clear messages for creation of trust.

Other issues from the planning stage are also important. For instance, in case an important goal of the merger is to acquire knowledge that in most cases is embedded in people and teams, the important issue is retaining key talents and top executives. As was described in earlier chapters, the two main factors that influence key talent turnover after the merger are the level of cultural differences and the level of integration. First, in some M&As, the agreement includes payment conditions upon retaining top executives and key talents. For instance, a certain percentage of the payment is held and transferred to the target firm owners, if all, or a certain percentage of, important people remain one or more years after the merger. Second, as administration experts, the HR managers will design an organizational structure that keeps as much autonomy as possible and suggests communication connections for the key talent and top executives in such a way that will keep them as long as needed after the M&A deal.

Implementation Stage

Maybe the greatest challenge facing top executives during the implementation stage is how to manage the transition from two organizations to one integrated company. During the PMI, different cultures and philosophies, organizational structures, systems, and processes are brought together. This requires that a plan and process has to be established and decisions have to be made to reconcile these differences so that potential synergies can be achieved. If left unattended with no systematic planning, clashes between firms will likely result, thus undermining the chances to realize synergy. Therefore, transition structure and integration approaches (see Chapter 13, "Integration Approaches") need to be planned and established. Furthermore, training and communication are needed to promote learning and joint problem-solving between executives and employees of the combined companies.

All issues of culture clashes and conflicts, control and evaluation of the behavioral side of people, especially at the target firm (overt conflicting behavior, health problems, absenteeism, turnover, and so on), creation of management transition structure, staffing, human capital integration, communication, leadership, and trust now largely depend on the HR department.

Another challenge for HR managers during PMI is how to combine the personnel policies and systems. These are of critical importance because of their direct effect on all employees and are likely to elicit strong reactions if there are changes, especially in ways that make them less attractive.

In many M&As, some reduction in force (RIF) might be needed. First, a decision about how to arrive at the RIF is important. Second, how to outplace employees must be determined. Many have argued that management should ease the RIF process by relying first on voluntary turnover programs such as early retirement incentives and attractive severance benefits, and by helping through the use of outplacement services such as in-house and external outplacement services, retraining employees, relocation to other jobs. However, these approaches have an effect on those who are terminated, and they also have an effect on those who remain. Those who stay watch how those who were terminated were let go. This provides retained employees with clear signals as to what they can expect in the future and what the company culture is actually like.

Employee perceptions of justice or fairness concerning how they are treated with regard to rewards, training, promotions, and other individual considerations have important consequences for the success of the PMI. Employees who feel that they are treated fairly and with respect are more inclined to exhibit high levels of commitment and organizational citizenship behaviors. This means that such employees will do things for the organization over and above that which they are contractually obliged to do.

It is inevitable that some managers and employees will be transferred during the integration process because both firms are often geographically separated. The selection of managers for overseas assignments who are open to new experiences, culturally sensitive, have linguistic skills, and attune to the normative patterns and rules of social engagement in the host country is important. Personal qualities such as patience, interpersonal tact, empathy, and a low need to control people and situations are also valuable. Sufficient support such as cost-of-living adjustments and mortgage buy downs can be good sources of motivation to transfer.

A number of programs, such as intercultural awareness training, stress management training, career counseling, and small group meetings can help employees cope with change. For example, communication and intercultural training can be necessary to prepare managers for interacting with employees who might be feeling angry, upset, and insecure, and who do not share the same culture. Similarly, retraining programs can help employees to develop new job skills. Training in conflict resolution and team-building can help managers and employees to deal with new work situations.

HR Practices

A firm that is better than its competitors, in the development of HR practices as a source of competitive advantage, employs people who are highly effective relative to the competition. It is argued that effective employees create superiority both in the primary value chain and in support activities. By extension, better practices and employees produce excellent knowledge and resource transfer and create knowledge of integration capabilities. The HR management strategy can be articulated as establishing policies that result in the creation of firm-specific, inimitable assets in the form of knowledge, skills, and abilities embedded in the human capital of the acquiring and acquired firms. Specific HR practices, such as training employees to deal with conflict and for new assignments during the integration period, using communication to address HR stress and uncertainty, and adjusting other (for example, recruiting, reward, and labor relations) practices to the new situation are indicators that the firm pursues a strategy likely to result in integration capabilities. The contention here is that the use of these practices and the results they produce are indicators that the firm has successfully created valuable assets in its people, assets that help integrate the two companies and improve financial performance.

There is no consensus on which HR practices are most important for improving performance. After analyzing many studies, the most commonly HR practices used are training, communication and information sharing, and involvement in decision making and autonomy (Weber, Rachman-Moore, and Tarba, 2012).

Training

Training and development are pivotal in the M&A for managing cross-cultural situations. Managers and employees need training to deal with various conflicts that result in HR problems. They must also meet the needs of new positions that are created, replace employees who leave after mergers, and adjust to work processes that are introduced. Research found that training programs conducted in the course of the M&A were positively associated with knowledge transfer (Weber, Rachman-Moore, and Tarba, 2012). Scholars concluded that an effective training system is an important mechanism in ensuring that employees have the necessary skills and add value to the company's success.

To develop an integration capability, employees of both companies involved in the merger must learn about the other company and its assets, people, structure, culture, HR practices, their own roles in transferring and coordinating specific resources across the two companies, the roles of others, and what the deliverables will be throughout the integration process. In addition, training is required for the M&A in general, and their own merger in particular, on such issues as the specific cultural differences in their particular merger, the effects of cultural differences on HR, managing resistance to change, dealing with conflict during the PMI, and more. Training helps to absorb knowledge in several ways, such as the use of databases and manuals, and helps develop processes and routines that encourage the use of acquired knowledge. Thus, training is essential for the effectiveness of the entire integration process.

Naturally, training programs conducted within the M&A context are in addition to the regular training needs of the companies and involve additional costs (travel, external providers, time, and more). The knowledge and experience of the people in each organization in the merger (the human capital) is a key factor in the creation of new practices and the improvement of existing ones. Moreover, training encourages managers and employees to look for new ways and practices for identifying the existence, location, and significance of new knowledge in the other party to the merger. Regardless of how extensive the due diligence process was, it is always necessary to continue training during the post-merger period to learn and teach about unexpected problems and conflicts and about coping with new challenges. Most of these investments in training often increase the firm's specificity in manager and employee skills and help develop integration capabilities.

References

Lubatkin, M., Schweiger, D., and Weber, Y. (1999). Top management turnover in related M&A's: An additional test of the theory of relative standing. *Journal of Management*, 25 (1), 55–73.

Gomes, E., Angwin, D., Weber, Y., and Tarba, S.Y. (2013). Critical success factors through the mergers and acquisitions process: Revealing pre- and post-M&A connections for improved performance. *Thunderbird International Business Review*, 55 (1), 13-35.

Weber, Y. and Tarba, S. Y. (2012). Cross-cultural analysis at mergers and acquisitions stages. *OD Practitioner (Special Issue on Organizational Develpments's Role in Improving Mergers and Acquisitions)*, 44 (3), 37-43.

Weber, Y. and Tarba, S.Y. (2010). Human resource practices and performance of mergers and acquisitions in Israel. *Human Resource Management Review*, 20, 203-211.

Weber, Y., Rachman-Moore, D., and Tarba, S. Y. (2012). Human resource practices during post-merger conflict and merger performance. *International Journal of Cross-Cultural Management*, 12 (1), 73-99.

Weber, Y. and Drori, I. (2011). Integrating organizational and human behavior perspectives on mergers and acquisitions: Looking inside the black box. *International Studies of Management & Organization*, 41 (3), 76-95.

15

M&A LEADERSHIP

Introduction

Looking at the M&A literature, it seems that leadership issues have taken a back seat in academic and practitioners' ideas and discussions (Gomes, Angwin, Weber, and Tarba, 2013). In most cases in which one points on M&A key success or failure factors, it is clear that sometimes leadership is mentioned but largely neglected. Over the last three decades, the discipline of strategic management has become increasingly concerned with top executives and their efforts to formulate strategy, but mentioned leadership issues only in passing. The M&A research (Gomes, Angwin, Weber, and Tarba, 2013) has not systematically examined leadership variables and referred to leadership issues only incidentally. Thus, current literature (Gomes, Weber, Brown, and Tarba, 2011) indicates that leadership is very essential for M&A process and success, but it is treated in a way that seems to reflect the need to acknowledge what is an obviously important factor, but does not address it substantively. However, research in recent years points to new finding about the roles and effects of leadership and trust in the M&A (Waldman and Javidan, 2009; Vasilaki, 2011). The purpose of this chapter is to fill this gap and describes leadership roles, skills, challenges, and necessary actions for M&A success.

Leadership Challenges During an M&A

There are many challenges to deal with during M&A stages. Here is a list to consider:

- Have a clear strategic rationale for the M&A.

- Make sure that all stakeholders clearly understand the rationale and the reasons for doing the deal, including strategic fit and the advantages for doing the M&A.

- Ensure that stakeholders supportive of the M&A will champion it and are committed to making it successful in the long run.

- Manage the interface between two organizations, especially the consequences of the contact between two national and organizational cultures.

- Win people over.

- Establish trust between the people of the two organizations on all levels.

- Manage the integration process to achieve the strategic goals of the M&A.

The Roles and Skills of Leadership in an M&A

Leadership is distinct from management, although you can fulfill both types of roles simultaneously. In M&As, leaders have unique roles that are different from typical managerial roles. They need to have good strategic thinking and visioning capabilities and a commitment to quickly and clearly inform the organization about how the integration process will unfold.

Leadership in the M&A involves not only the management of two organizations, but also the interface between them, including the contact between two cultures. The latter is the biggest challenge. This requires team leadership and collaboration skills, good planning capabilities, abilities to gain trust, the willingness and motivation of managers and employees to deal with difficulties, and changing situations and uncertainties about the business situations and one's future career.

An essential role in the M&A involves the implementation of the post-merger integration (PMI) process. This includes, among other things, the selection of an integration manager, establishment of the executive teams that will guide the PMI, active change in leadership, handling of conflicts between people from both sides, coordination of all integration activities, and more.

The objectives of the integration process follow:

- Create organizational readiness for the M&A.

- Get the full picture about issues that were not completed prior to the closing.

- Integrate smoothly to seize synergies.

- Rebuild the organization as an entity that can realize financial strategic objectives.

- Build the unified culture with common values that are necessary for knowledge sharing between the two organizations.

- Transfer best practices and important knowledge between the two organizations.

- Overcome all challenges of culture clash and change management.

The accomplishment of these objectives usually requires the following activities:

- Communicate the leader's vision for the new organization.

- Finalize all planning and analytical activities that were not accomplished before the closing.

- Build teams that will guide the PMI.

- Achieve cultural integration.

- Assimilate new managers and people.

- Establish a communication strategy.

- Handle staffing and organizational structure plans.

- Ensure human capital integration.

Leadership Teams

As indicated, one of the most challenging tasks is to create effective teams that will manage the PMI process. The transfer of knowledge from one acquisition to the next would require that certain leaders remain with the organization and also relates to the creation of specific teams to handle the acquisition and its integration as discussed in chapters 2 and 3.

In the process of bringing together different countrywide sales organizations through acquiring dealers and merging them, the Toyota Industries Corporation created teams that worked with the national representatives to transfer knowledge between the individual acquisitions, for instance. And companies, such as Company A in Sweden, might well establish a separate organization to deal with acquisition issues. These organizations, or the management representatives engaging with the national leaders, need to ensure that leaders also obtain such knowledge because this would help them in the future.

The leadership team also needs to be of a certain size. This allows for individual members to contribute with their specific, in-depth knowledge, rather than broad and more general knowledge. The integration of companies is a complex task, and therefore the more people, the easier to handle upcoming conflicts and discuss them. Too many leaders can increase the complexity without adding to the output, so although the team needs to be of a certain size, it needs to be balanced so that each party actually has something to contribute. This, in turn, relates to the next aspect: It is critical how the management team is put together.

Diverse experiences, educational backgrounds, and firm tenure are expected to all positively contribute to the outcome of the M&A. Such diversity among team members helps them to understand different issues, and also means that they have a better understanding for the target company's circumstances. As in any team building, the individual members' diversity should not be too large, however, because this will inhibit their interaction. A certain overlap of knowledge is required so that the team members can communicate effectively with one another. Together with the size of the team, this thus means that an optimal amount of team members with overlapping yet diverse competencies should be created. The size of the team would in the end relate to the complexity of the task. The more complex the acquisition (in terms of bringing together parties from different countries bringing together large companies, including companies from diverse areas, and entailing a high degree of integration), the larger the team.

Leadership Skills

Important leadership skills are those of managing group processes, collaborative skills, and motivating managers and employees. This links to how the leaders are those that guide the employees' future activities. This does not only require the actual task-related integration of companies, but also social integration of people. Trust needs to be created among employees of both organizations, and that trust needs to include the trust of leaders, the trust of the staff of the other organization, and the trust of the overall integration process. In such endeavors, communication is essential. This applies to how to inform the staff and to create room for communication among employees and middle management. The leaders hence need to teach middle management how to communicate and work with those initiatives that the leaders bring forth. Communication is also important to create shared understandings on matters, as is the social integration to create trust and willingness to adjust and establish a common ground for future development of the organization. The integration thereby aims to create commitment among the staff of both organizations, and internalize values and goals so as they align, not only on a company level, they are also well spread and understood among employees.

The need for charismatic leadership is underlined in the post-merger phase. This describes how the leaders need to be visionary and forward-looking. The charismatic style further enables the spread of such visions to employees and the ability to convince people about the ideas for the future. This would help in the integration of firms and the unification of staff. Charismatic leadership could be described as personal characteristics and social skills, thus pointing to how the leader either portrays a certain leadership style based on her own merits and interests, or she can pursue changes that act on the level of socialization. The leader needs to have skills in formulating a vision for the future and making the organization work according to it (that is, commit to it), which requires those latter skills. Personalized charisma will lead to absorption strategies and cause stress within the organization. Socialized charisma is needed to create a collaborative atmosphere and make people commit to the new organization. The following section describes transformational leadership in more detail.

Various leadership attributes explain how leadership affects change processes. Sitkin and Pablo (2004) suggest a six-dimension integrative model of leadership that can be applied to pre- and post-acquisition stages. This model shows how each attribute affects followers. *Inspirational leadership* involves the commitment of the leader to attaining challenging goals and influencing aspiration of followers. It refers to building the desire for excellence by raising expectations, enthusiasm, and confidence. Thus, this attribute is an important influence during alliances because it determines the direction of the newly combined entity. *Contextual leadership* refers to the creation of conditions that enable managers and employees to focus and be effective. Here the leader is a chief community builder in the post-merger stage that creates the necessary organization's structure, process, and culture. For example, the leader redesigns rules, goals, procedures, policies, and measures, thus, providing a road map to help members see the work ahead. It means also establishing success factors consistent with the new organization strategy and adhering to the new culture.

Personal leadership creates loyalty and concerns with the leaders being role models for organizational members. This attribute can be a strong force in helping the new entity adjust to the actualities of post-merger requirements. *Relational leadership* involves the leader forging strong ties with individuals in the organizations and influencing a sense of trust and justice. It is essential for the integration process to include a transitional stage during which employees are prepared for the knowledge and capabilities of the transfer. This attribute helps create an atmosphere in which there is mutual understanding and a willingness to participate in organizational building.

Supportive leadership refers to making organizational members aware of the pressing organizational problems and challenges and making them secure enough to take appropriate corrective actions. Through the change situation, people go through a number of stages, including denial, acknowledgment, and acceptance. The individual ability to deal with risk and associated fear depend on his confidence and desire for opportunity-seeking. The supportive leadership throughout the M&A process involves making organizational members feel secure enough to take risks by fostering a sense of acceptance, personal efficacy, confidence, and willingness to rely on collective understanding. Finally, *stewardship leadership* involves the leader acting as steward of the institution, honoring and protecting deeply held values. In the integration process, leaders must play the role of chief integrator and balancer, ensuring that the multiple elements of leadership described here are drawn together and weighted most effectively for the particular situation.

Transformational Leadership

One of the emergent concepts in leadership in general, and in M&As, is *transformational leadership*. It is the ability to inspire and stimulate others to change. It refers to the leader's ability to provide an appealing vision for the merger and alliances, inspire and motivate employees and managers to achieve the alliance goals, and challenge followers to develop creative solutions to the problems that might arise during the integration process. For example, to transfer capabilities and know-how between the organizations in the alliance, leaders need to create the right atmosphere that stimulates bilateral cultural and organizational understanding and mutual willingness to cooperate.

Transformational leadership includes motivation to inspire, considerations on individual levels, and stimulation. Intellectual stimulation would be the most important feature. It links to how culture is taught by the leadership and adopted by other organizational members. Such leaders have a clear idea on where they want to take the combined organization, while they also are oriented to do the best for the organization rather than for themselves. For the organizational members, they would identify with the leader, while also regarding him as a role model. Transformational leadership is related to how the organizational members learn to adapt to the new situation and contribute to the overall goal. This, in turn, suggests a leadership style that is not direct, but visionary and embedding. Goal clarity and the creation of a creative organizational climate are items related to transformational leadership. The organizational climate describes the context of individuals' activities and is oriented to the organizational circumstances, rather than underlying values of the organization. Densten (2008) describes how one leadership skill is to create an organizational climate that allows for staff to be creative and flexible, while it is also important that they follow overall directions. An open climate allows for the individual employees to create their own understanding of the new situation and thereby embrace it, rather than push ideas on them, while the overall direction remains explicit. This in turn creates a culture that is open to change and that enables adjustment and learning by its members. Employees trusting the organization and its intentions further means that they feel freer to contribute to ideas and be creative, something that will benefit the new organization. Employee anxiety has been extensively reported following a merger or acquisition, and a leadership style that reduces any such type of anxiety is valuable for the organization and the outcome of the M&A. This, in turn, means that employees receive clarity and also are expected to obtain a positive attitude to the M&A. Unsatisfied staff might choose to leave the company and work against overall directions and intentions. Also, their overall effectiveness in their jobs might decrease if they are uncertain about the future or do not feel that the future organization fits with their goals or even acts hostile to them.

The effects of transformational leadership can be described as creating the acceptance for the acquisition, enhancing performance, and increasing job satisfaction. Each item is essential on the short- and long-run for the success of the M&A. For the short-run success, it is important that employees commit to the acquisition to work in accordance with its implementation. It is also important that operational work runs as before because an M&A can create a critical interruption in these regards, where competitors can grasp opportunities, not the least in terms of sales. In the long-term perspective, it is vital that staff continue with the firm because they often are valuable knowledge bases and also because they know present routines and ways to conduct business. In addition, they create contacts to such external parties as customers and suppliers. For staff to stay on, job satisfaction is important, while the commitment to the acquisition is necessary to make them work in accordance with the intentions of owners and managers. The transformational leadership includes the ability to create a creative work environment. This, in turn, leads to the renewal of the organization, and further means that staff expectedly remains more satisfied with their work because it allows them to develop in their positions and add to the company, and also means that they become more open to the newness of the combined firm.

In Toyota Industries' acquisition of the forklift manufacturer BT Industries, Toyota for a long time kept the acquired party as a sovereign unit. In the latter stage of PMI, much freedom was retained. The climate that was created was one that would allow for employees to create their own space and adapt the organization to local circumstances. Much of the integration relied on local staff because Toyota had first pointed out goals and communicated these to employees and middle management.

Vasilaki (2011) describes transformational leadership in relation to different degrees of integration. Transformational leadership is needed regardless of the degree of integration but would act in different ways for it. The idealizing influencing would need to be more predominant if the companies are to be integrated, while the consideration on individual levels is as important regardless of the degree of integration. This relates to how transformational leadership either is focused at reassuring staff that nothing will change and that it will be business as usual, or how the leadership aims to transform the values of the staff and make them open to change.

Densten (2008) refers to organizational climates at different stages of the integration and points to certain shifts in the balance between direction and an open-oriented organizational climate. In the initial phase of integration, anxiety among staff will be predominant. In that phase, clarity about visions is needed, as is the creation of enthusiasm for the integration. Focus should be on influencing rather than controlling. As the actual integration is put into motion, there will be "real" problems to solve that previously have only been anticipated by staff. As a consequence, leaders should become increasingly direct to decrease confusion and to make this critical phase run as smoothly as possible, with as few interruptions internally and externally as could be accomplished. Leadership should thereby be more direct than in the initial phase. The clarification of goals continues to be important, but also the distribution of roles, the implementation of motivations, and personal drives among employees. Hence, leaders should be clear, but this is not synonymous with acting without regard to the employees. Manifestation of goals, clear communication, and clarity in terms of the operationalization of goals are important. As employees become introduced to their new roles, suggestions are that the leadership style should once again promote an increasingly open organizational climate. Leaders should coordinate and monitor, while not be directly involved in the operational aspects. Following the integration, there can be some kind of aftermath effect to the integration. They can follow from mistakes or inabilities to actually get the staff to commit to the integration and new organization. This phase could largely be avoided through the correct handling of staff, but should issues occur, it is critical to practice a leadership style that captures any such difficulties, communicates, and listens to the staff and their concerns.

Unifying Culture

Although any operational change is not simple to acquired people, in cultural change, employees become aware that organizational life, measuring tools for performance, processes and procedures, and loyalty have changed suddenly. This threat to long accepted organizational values and beliefs creates cultural shock, loss of identity, and low levels of trust.

It is not surprising, therefore, that corporate leaders often encounter strong resistance to their efforts to redirect the acquired company and the related cultural change. The attempt to change organizational culture to a different value and belief system that is also related to identity change is probably the hardest of all challenges facing any manager in M&A and alliances (Weber and Drori, 2011). Thus, what some corporate executives face is that good public relations are clearly not enough to deal with the acquired management and employees' reaction to change.

On one hand, poor performance of acquisitions is attributed, among other things, to a void of leadership during the integration process. On the other hand, recent research findings give support to the notion that leadership attributes can enhance post-acquisition performance and can moderate the negative effects of culture clash on performance (Vasilaki, 2011). Leadership can facilitate PMI through leadership processes that create, change, integrate, and embody culture manifestation (Bligh, 2006). Furthermore, leaders provide vision and inspiration to their followers and create a structure and a culture that can enable and facilitate various positive behaviors that are essential for integrating the two organizations. For example, goal clarity and support for creative thinking was found to improve performance and job satisfaction in M&As (Nemanich and Keller, 2007).

The unification of culture between the acquirer and the acquired party can mean that values from one party are transferred to the other organization, or it can describe how a new culture is created out of previous ones, or with new values added. In the instance in which companies want to integrate on equal terms rather than have the acquirer (or potentially reverse) take over the acquired party, the unification of culture is important. This means that a new culture is created based on visions about how the future company should look and based on input from both sides.

The organizational climate focuses on the practice of the organizations, while culture describes their values. Culture (and climate) are closely related to leadership style. Leaders can enable or inhibit individuals' change acceptance. In accordance with the transformational leadership style that allows for individuals to shape their own understanding, this is also important to accomplish cultural change. Support-oriented leadership, rather than direct leadership built only on power, is important to accomplish cultural change among employees. In the unification of culture, the socialized charisma of leaders is important, as it allows for the collaborative vision and the genuine commitment of parties as outcome.

However, a shift in culture and the re-orientation of tasks will affect different employees differently. This both relates to how they might find the situation more or less stressful, but also that they are actually more or less affected by the integration. In the unidirectional unification of culture, and the unidirectional integration of firms, it would foremost be members of the acquired organization that need to change and its empoyees will experience the stress from it. For instance, following the Finnish company BasWare's acquisition of the Swedish firm Momentum Doc, it was foremost the staff of Momentum Doc that experienced changes. They found themselves subordinated, and reactions included staff leaving the organization.

Important features of the cultural leadership are to recognize pre-integration differences, work for the actual integration also on operational levels, collaborate with employees in the PMI, create realistic expectations, and work on symbolism to transfer values of individuals. Bligh (2006) describes this as the following themes: i) Leadership that creates in terms of recognizing historical cultural differences; providing outlets for loss and renewal; fostering realistic expectations of both challenges and opportunities. ii) Leadership that changes: articulating an ideology for change; creating ongoing momentum for the change process; utilizing the symbolism of the mundane; and role modeling a commitment to the change process. iii) Leadership that integrates: actively team-building across previous site memberships; utilizing employee input into the post-merger changes; and communicating informally about cultural differences. The cultural leadership operates on all levels of the organization, which partly separates it from transformational leadership as previously described. It is also explicit in the recognition of the change to create common grounds for change and realize what would be perceived as change and not change. Transformational leadership would work on the overall company level, whereas cultural leadership much more needs to be operationalized and represented by middle management. It is further more focused on the disbanding from previous views and values and engages more in the integration. Hence, transformational leadership might well be complemented by middle management working on cultural leadership.

In M&A, it is essential not to neglect leadership on the middle management and operational levels. The transformational, charismatic leader should guide those other leaders, specifically in terms of goal clarification and mentorship. This is so that the overall company vision becomes incorporated at operational levels, and to develop those leaders to be role models for their staff. Support to solve conflicts and guidance in how to accomplish goal fulfilment are important tasks in the transfer of leadership knowledge and style between top and middle management. To help the implementation of the vision, inscriptions in terms of rules, guiding documents, budgets, and other organizational artifacts can help (Öberg, Henneberg, and Mouzas, 2012). Their reasons are not to be the direct descriptions of work routines, but to guide work through providing structure and make it easier for staff to work in compliance with goals, rather than to find solutions that do not fit with the overall goal structure. Such guidance can include the implementation of certain report structures, key ratios, or ICT systems that guide work in specific flows or directions.

In the international M&A, the unification of cultures is increasingly complicated. This is due to how it not only represents differences between organizations, but also national differences that can impact how businesses are performed, understandings of communication patterns, and so forth. Also, transformational leadership helps in bringing organizations together. Individual considerations, intellectual stimulation, and idealized behavior will create advantages for the organization, and the charismatic leader is needed to enable transferring values and solving conflicts. This applies also to bringing together cultures from different nations.

References

Bligh, M.C. (2006). Surviving post-merger 'culture clash': Can cultural leadership lessen the causalities? *Leadership*, 2, 395-426.

Densten, I.L. (2008). How climate and leadership can be used to create actionable knowledge during stages of mergers and acquisitions. *Advances in Mergers and Acquisitions*, 7, 93-117.

Gomes, E., Angwin, D., Weber, Y., and Tarba, S.Y. (2013). Critical success factors through the mergers and acquisitions process: Revealing pre- and post-M&A connections for improved performance. *Thunderbird International Business Review*, 55 (1), 13-35.

Gomes, E., Weber, Y., Brown, C., and Tarba, S.Y. (2011). Mergers, acquisitions and strategic alliances: *Understanding the process*. USA & UK: Palgrave Macmillan.

Nemanich, L.A. and Keller, R.T. (2007). Transformational leadership in an acquisition: A field study of employees. *The Leadership Quarterly*, 18, 49-68.

Öberg, C., Henneberg, S.C., & Mouzas, S. (2012). Organizational inscriptions of network pictures: A meso-level analysis. *Industrial Marketing Management*.

Sitkin, S. B. and Pablo, A. L. (2005). The neglected importance of leadership in mergers and acquisitions. In: G. K. Stahl & M. E. Mendenhall (Eds), *Mergers and acquisitions: Managing culture and human resource*. Stanford: Stanford University Press.

Vasilaki, A. (2011). The relationship between transformational leadership and post-acquisition performance. *International Studies of Management & Organization*, 41 (3), 42-58.

Waldman, D.A. and Javidan, M. (2009). Alternative forms of charismatic leadership in the integration of mergers and acquisitions. *The Leadership Quarterly*, 20, 130-142.

Weber, Y. and Drori, I. (2011). Integrating organizational and human behavior perspectives on mergers and acquisitions: Looking inside the black box. *International Studies of Management & Organization*, 41 (3), 76-95.

16

TRUST FORMATION AND CHANGE IN M&A

Introduction

Trust is an essential component in all social exchange relationships. Executives and employees often find that the level of interpersonal trust is low in many organizations, and in M&As, it has many times deteriorated. Although control and legal mechanisms are adopted as substitutes to restore sufficient trust to necessary activities, in the M&A, much higher levels of trust are needed to deal with resistance to change and to overcome HR problems to successfully implement the post-merger integration (PMI) process. The development of trust and distrust and their effects on M&A performance have not been well articulated in current literature. The aim of this chapter is to describe in more details the role, antecedents, and outcomes of trust in M&A. Moreover, these details can help in the process of the formation, maintenance, change, dissolution, and possible repair of trust.

Trust in the M&A

It is surprising that trust has received so little attention in the literature on M&As in spite of its apparent coexistence with deception. When trust is noted, it is treated in an almost offhand way that reflects the need to acknowledge it. At the same time, trust can be mentioned as an important factor, while sidestepping the need to address it substantively and elaborating on its role in the M&A.

The important role of trust has been usually indicated when focusing on the negative effects of the M&A in the context of PMI. However, although the academic and practitioner M&A literature refers to trust, the specific mechanism by which M&A executives and employees use it has not been systematically explored by either practitioners or scholars.

The Nature of Trust

Trust affects almost every aspect of life in organizations. Here are some examples that are relevant to M&A:

- Enables cooperative behavior
- Promotes adaptive organizational forms
- Reduces harmful conflict
- Deceases transaction costs
- Promotes effective response to crisis

Most descriptions of trust focus on two main concepts:

- **Reliance on the other party**—This is a psychological state that is followed by actions in which one group or individuals permit their fate to be determined by another group or individual. In an M&A, the people of the acquired company become vulnerable to the leaders, managers, and employees of the buying firm.

- **Risk**—This describes a situation that the trusting party, target, or buying company people will experience negative outcomes if the other party proves untrustworthy.

These two concepts taken together imply that trust is based on the assessment of one party's competencies, integrity, and benevolence by another party and the costs of putting its fate in the hand of that party. The effects of these components can influence overall trust in various ways. It is possible that the components of perceived trustworthiness combine multiplicatively in determining overall trust, or a certain level of trust can develop with lower degrees of one or more of the components.

The trust assessment might depend on a prejudiced opinion and on actions taken by one party or both. Thus, trust should be viewed as a dynamic and evolving rather than a static phenomenon. Further, trust depends on mutual understanding and time. The experiences of success, failure, and interactions will influence the level of trust. Unlike many commodities, over the life of the relationships, trust can grow or wear out through use. Over time, as each partner learns about the other, the level of interorganizational trust will change. The important implication for M&A is that one party can take actions that shape and modify the interorganizational group and individual relationships.

The following points sum up some characteristics of the nature of trust:

- Trust is not a behavior but an underlying psychological condition.
- Trust changes over time; it can develop, build, decline, and even resurface in long-standing relationships.

- Trust has been found to be an important predictor of successful negotiations.

- In ongoing relationships, the question is not so much "How much do I trust?" but "In what areas and in what ways do I trust?"

- Interorganizational and interpersonal trust can be different because the focal object differs.

The following sections describe the components of the trust dynamic process that includes the formation, maintenance, change, dissolution, and possible repair of trust.

Several factors influence the level of trust and include, among other things, prior relationships, negotiation process, cultural differences, and an integration approach that influences the level of autonomy removed from the acquired management. Each contact brings some details that influence the learning process of one partner of the other party and will change the level of trust.

Prior Relationships

Any history of relationships between top executives, or any organizational unit, of the buying firm with the target firm will influence the perception that the other is trustworthy or not. Experienced partners can have a different relationship-building process than partners working together for the first time. Consider, for instance, the relationship between a supplier and customer that might enter into a vertical integration merger. The history of the relationship allows each side the opportunity to evaluate the future actions of the other party and its willingness and abilities to fulfill its promises.

The length of time and the intensity of prior relationships also influence the level of trust developed. Longer and more intensive relationships usually have passed through conflicts and influence attempts by both partners. Thus, longer relationships between the suppliers and customers can bring higher familiarity and understanding about each other with knowledge of the other's procedures and values. If the relationship were successful in the past and each perceives one another as complying with norms of equity, there is a higher chance for development of a higher level of trust and vice versa.

Finally, personal relationships between executives from both partners can serve to shape the trust between the partner firms and thus should be viewed as critical in establishment of trust and repair in case trust was deteriorated. After all, the individual relationship and personal bonds of friendship foster trust by building one-on-one relationships with the partners. For example, one factor that led to good trust development in the merger between Procter & Gamble and Gillette was that both CEOs, Lafley and Kilts, knew each other. They both served on the board of the Grocery Manufacturer's Association. In the case of P&G and Gillette, the two CEOs evaluated how much they could cooperate with the other CEO based on information and judgments they made about the other party's credibility.

Negotiation Process

Chapter 8, "Selection of Target and Negotiation Process," highlights the importance of building a good relationship between the partners that is based on trust. This is critical because the end stage of deal agreement represents the beginning of the next stage in which both parties will start working together. Thus, a high level of trust can be achieved when each party tries to safeguard not only their own interests but also the interests of the other party. Gillette's CEO, Kilts, assumed that Lafley would want to include bankers and lawyers, but Lafley communicated that he trusted him enough to not bring in these early stage consultants, which could have a negative impact on the trust they had begun to build.

Partner Abilities and Competencies

In an M&A, trust is based also on the risk associated with the reliance of one party on the other party. In other words, the acquiring management has to rely on the target management to perform critical tasks. Thus, the buying management must believe that the acquired management has both the desire and abilities to achieve the goals of the merger. Without such belief, it will be impossible to develop trust. Therefore, trust can be developed after an assessment of the target firm's skills and competencies. In some cases, this assessment will take into account the target firm's reputation. The aforementioned assessment and level of trust will be associated with the level of autonomy removal from acquired management that, in turn, can lead to conflict, turnover, and other behavioral problems.

Cultural Differences

As was described in detail in Chapter 6, "Culture and Cultural Differences Analysis," the amount of cultural differences can influence the communication problems between the two parties. Furthermore, differences in belief values and managerial philosophies and preferences can have a major impact on trust. The higher the cultural differences and the higher the communication problems, the lower will be the level of trust. First, the risk associated with the cross-cultural relationships will influence the level of trust not only because of lack of understanding and familiarity but also because of uncertainty about opportunistic behavior. Second, when one side does not share the values of the other side, trust will erode again for lack of understanding. In such cases in M&As, cultural stereotypes develop and further fuel feelings of hostility and mistrust.

Leadership

Related to leadership described in Chapter 15, "M&A Leadership," how representatives of one organization or the other one communicate relies on the leaders. This is essential also for PMI expectations because it means that those other parties hope for a leader who has their best interests in mind, in addition to his efforts to accomplish strategy and vision. Charismatic leadership would enable such a creation of trust, but trust can also follow from continuous work, in which the employee is eventually confident to trust the new organization and its leaders. Leaders that are open in their communication and that are also clear in their vision can speed up any such process. These continuous experiences, other processes such as communication, and learning processes on both sides that influence the evolution of trust are the subjects of the next sections.

Process Dynamic and Learning

Contact between the two parties will influence the evolution of trust between them. Managers and employees watch each partner's decisions and actions, learn about the other, and arrive to conclusions that can increase, or deteriorate, the level of trust that is based on initial conditions. During the mutual learning process, each partner understands better the goals, strategic intentions, culture, complementary contributions, benefits, and processes that take place at the PMI stage. Such actions and decisions and their influence on trust are described next.

Communication

Communication is pivotal in the evolution of trust. As indicated, understanding and familiarity are essential for trust development. Communication that reduces uncertainty and clarifies intentions and processes can increase trust between the parties. Chapter 12, "Communication," describes in detail the advantage, process, media, and strategy of communication, which all are key factors in building trust.

Communication can decrease stress and anxiety and build credibility on both sides. Target managers and employees are usually concerned about their new roles, tasks, job security, and benefits following the merger. Communication can help to mitigate suspicion and increase commitment to the success of the M&A. Poor communication can reduce trust and increase rumors and turnover of key talent and top executives of the target firm.

Part of communication is the transfer of knowledge that can help to realize synergy and contribute to the benefits that each party can earn by getting skills from the other party. The knowledge can be internalized by each partner and applied to current and new products and geographic markets as well as to any units and functions in organizations such as marketing, HR, logistics, R&D, finance, and so on. Such benefits can increase the trust that each firm's members have in the other partner, its competencies and benefits to the success of the M&A.

Autonomy Removal

The buying firm typically imposes control and coordination measures on the acquired managers and employees to realize the expected synergy and to ensure that goals and strategies are achieved and that the M&A operates in a manner consistent with the buyer's culture and standards. The related autonomy removal that is necessary for the realization of synergy can be devastating for the managers of the target firm and usually is followed by stress and negative attitudes that lead to lower commitment to the success of the M&A, and lower cooperation of the acquired managers with the acquiring managers in both domestic and international M&As (Weber et al., 1996; Weber and Drori, 2011). In some M&As, this can lead to high turnover among acquired top executives as well as affect overall M&A performance.

These outcomes, in turn, influence trust. The removal of autonomy can be perceived as absence of trust. Further, it can result in resistance and conflicts that can bring about a cycle of escalating distrust. This occurs when each side adjusts its assessment of the other side's trustworthiness following the actions and conflicts.

If the control mechanisms lead to knowledge transfer, well communicated and rewarded, and good performance results, the process of balanced autonomy removal can increase trust. Furthermore, when sides develop mutual trust, there can be a lower need for control and coordination. Acquired managers can receive more autonomy and new tasks that can result in escalation of higher trust.

Perceived Benefits

Chapter 14, "Human Capital Issues and Practices," focused on HR practices and the "me" issue for each individual in M&As, especially at the acquired company. Thus, the opportunities for new jobs, increased salary, and growth can bring a higher level of trust, while a threat on job security, changes, and lower salaries can bring distrust. Thus, personal benefits, opportunities, or losses attributed to the merger are key factors in the evolution of trust.

Consequences of the M&A and Trust

Trust seems to ensure sound and cooperative relationships between the managers and employees of both parties in M&As. The consequences of high trust summarized by Weber et al. (2013) follow:

- Lower stress and anxiety
- Prevention of the typical negative attitudes toward the merger
- Prevention of the typical negative attitudes toward the buying company and its management

- High level of commitment to the success of the merger

- High level of cooperation of the target firm's members and acquiring management and employees

- Lower turnover than usual in the M&A

- Higher M&A performance than those cases with a low level of trust

Recent findings (for example, Stahl et al., 2011) confirmed that most of the initial conditions influence the level of trust, as suggested earlier in this chapter, and also most of the consequences of trust.

References

Stahl, G. K., Chua, C. H. and Pablo, A. L. (2012). Does national context affect target firm employees' trust in acquisitions? *Management International Review*, 52 (3), 395-423.

Stahl, G. K., Larsson, R., Kremershof, I. and Sitkin, S.B. (2011). Trust dynamics in acquisitions: A case survey. *Human Resource Management*, 50, 575–603.

Stahl, G. K. and Sitkin, S. B. (2010). Trust dynamics in acquisitions: The role of relationship history, interfirm distance, and acquirer's integration approach. *Advances in Mergers & Acquisitions*, 9, 51-82.

Weber, Y., Drori, I., and Tarba, S.Y. (2013). Culture-performance relationships in international mergers and acquisition: The role of trust. *European Journal of Cross-Cultural Competence and Management*, 2 (3/4), 252-274.

Index

I

Icarus, 6
identification
    criteria, 86-94
    process of, 83-86
implementation of HR issues, 184
improvement of competitive
  advantages, 64
increase in M&A activities, 5
independent search plans, 92
indexes for control, 26
infrastructure integration, 23
innovation, approaches to, 73
innovation-intensive acquisitions, 59
inspirational leadership, 192
integration
    approaches to, 25, 167
    cultural, 24
    culture clashes, 167-168
    frameworks, 172-174
    horizontal, 44-45
    human capital, 22-23, 177-178
        cultural differences, 178-180
        HR issues, 181, 184
        practices, 185
        training, 186
    model for value creation, 17-26
    planning, 20
    PMI, 190
    post-merger integration (PMI), 16,
     40-41
    processes, 9
    stages, 14-17
    synergy exploitation, 168, 172
    vertical, 45-47, 62-65
interdependence, lateral, 73

internal parties, communications with,
  160-163
interpretations, 72
interrelationships, 14-17
investments
    banking, 24
    budgets, 93
    requirements, evaluation of, 106-107
iPods, 45

J–K

Jaguar, 106-108
Jeep, 32
joint ventures, 47-48

Kentucky Fried Chicken, 64
knowledge accumulation,
  encouragement of, 85
knowledge transfers, 54-61, 191

L

Land Rover, 106
Lannet, 9
lateral interdependence, 73
lawyers, 147
leadership, 189
    CEOs. *See* CEOs
    challenges during an M&A, 189
    culture clash
        managing, 153-156
        overview of, 151-152
    culture clashes, 167-168
    evaluation of, 107
    human capital, 177-178
        cultural differences, 178-180
        HR issues, 181, 184

communication with stakeholders, 158
  external parties, 158-160
  internal parties, 160-163
  managing, 163-166
decision making, 74
due diligence, 127-128
  business/operational, 132-135
  cultures, 136-137
  Do's and Don'ts, 140
  extension of examination, 128-129
  legal topics, 130-132
  synergies, 137-139
integrated model for value creation, 17-26
knowledge transfer, 56
negotiations, 20-21, 109-114, 119-122
PMI, 190
search and identification, 83-94
strategic decisions, 37
  choice of partners, 40-41
  diversification, 41
  emergent/planned strategies, 37-40
  entering new industries, 41-48
trust, 205-206
products, cross-selling, 31
profiles, short-listed companies, 102
profitability, 91
profits
  lack of, 6
  stockholders, 5
  warnings, 3
progress, tracking, 26
psychological contracts between employers and employees, 15
purchase of AMC by Chrysler, 32
putdowns, 153

Q–R

quality of management teams, 106

ratios, valuation, 32
realization, 53
records, tracking, 26
reduction in force. *See* RIF
related diversification, 43-47
relational leadership, 193
relationships, 14-17
  government, 38
  horizontal, 73
  trust, 203, 206-207
reliance on other parties (trust), 202
removal of autonomy, 206
re-orientation of tasks, 197
requirements of investments, 108-109
research, sources of information (screening), 105
resources, sharing, 54-61
reviewing due diligence, 128-129
rewards, approaches to, 75
RIF (reduction in force), 184
rights, voting, 142
risk-taking, approaches to, 73
risk (trust), 202
roles
  leadership, 190-198
  of trust, 201-204
roof (of deals), 111
Russo, Patricia, 3

S

satisfaction of management, 16
saving on expenses, 63
Schrempp, Juergen, 10

turnover, 14-16
    programs, 184
    top executives, 14
Tyco, 42
types
    of knowledge, 55
    of leadership, 193

U

uncertainty avoidance (UA), 173
unifying cultures, 196-197
Unilever, 3
unrelated diversification, 42

V

valuation, 15
    price, 109
    ratios, strategic motives for M&A, 32
    of transactions (LOIs), 142
value-added chain, 46
values
    creation
        integrated model for, 17-26
        motives, 30
    culture clash, 152
    effect on stocks, 5
variables, 14
ventures, joint, 47-48
vertical acquisitions, 88
vertical integration, 18, 45-47, 62-65
volume, global volume of M&A
  activity, 4
voluntary turnover programs, 184
voting rights, 142

W–Z

warnings, profits, 3
WilmerHale report (2012), 4
workers' agreements, 143

Yoplait, 64

FINANCIAL TIMES

In an increasingly competitive world, it is quality
of thinking that gives an edge—an idea that opens new
doors, a technique that solves a problem, or an insight
that simply helps make sense of it all.

We work with leading authors in the various arenas
of business and finance to bring cutting-edge thinking
and best-learning practices to a global market.

It is our goal to create world-class print publications
and electronic products that give readers
knowledge and understanding that can then be
applied, whether studying or at work.

To find out more about our business
products, you can visit us at www.ftpress.com.